DISCC

WHEN YOU GO THROUGH THE DARK SEASONS

HOPE

IS

ALWAYS

REAL

DORRIS WALKER-TAYLOR

Change Her Story
c/o Her Purpose Press
1703 N McMullen Booth Road #201
Safety Harbor, FL 34695
info@changeherstory.org
Scriptures are taken from:

Holman Christian Standard Bible (HCSB)

Copyright @ 1999, 2000, 2002, 2003, 2009 by Holman Bible Publishers, Nashville Tennessee. All rights reserved.

King James Version Public Domain, Bible Gateway

New American Standard Bible (NASB)

Copyright @ 1960, 1962, 1963, 1968, 1971, 1972, 1973, 1975, 1977, 1995 by The Lockman Foundation

New International Version (NIV)

Holy Bible, New International Version®, NIV® Copyright @1973, 1978, 1984, 2011 by Biblica, Inc.® Used by permission. All rights reserved worldwide.

ISBN: 978-1- 951781-12-5

Printed in USA

DEDICATION

First and foremost, thank you, heavenly Father, for never leaving me nor forsaking me.

To my children, Sonya Hall and Clifford Walker: I love you and will never leave you again until the Lord comes to take me home.

To my sister Portia: I love you. Please start living before you die.

To my brother James: I love you dearly. I pray for your healing daily.

To Mom and Dad: I'm married now and doing so much better in life. Thank you both for the awareness of God and legacy of faith.

To Becca Stevens: Thank you for the community of Thistle Farms you birthed. I love you.

To the love of my life, James Taylor, my husband: I love you and adore the way you treat me. Thank you for bringing joy, hope, and love into my life.

Contents

FOREWORD

I met Dorris Walker in 2009 when she came to live in Magdalene House—a community of women committed to live together to escape lives of addiction and prostitution. While she was on the streets of Nashville, Dorris endured unspeakable violence and trauma. Addicted to drugs, turning tricks for money, and sleeping in alleys, she arrived exhausted in body, mind, and soul.

She found rest at Magdalene, the residential program of Thistle Farms, where she got clean and sober and received the medical and dental care, counseling, and education she needed to be freed of her addiction. She quickly became known for her kindness, her contagious optimism, and her beautiful singing voice. She remains a highly valued member of the team at Thistle Farms. For more than a decade she's represented us at events across the country.

Most importantly, Dorris is my friend. And I love her.

Thistle Farms's residential program welcomes and cares for women wounded in body and soul. Their history of abuse has stolen all sense of their incredible worth. Their heartbreaking tragic stories can be overwhelming. The evil I've heard and seen, things I wish I didn't know, would make your skin crawl. Other stories of

1

redemption and God's faithfulness make me smile so big my face hurts. Like the time my friend Dorris first saw the ocean.

She and I were scheduled at an event in Florida where I'd speak and she'd manage the table where we sold products made by the Thistle Farms residents. Having always lived in Tennessee, Dorris had never seen the ocean, and we were determined to make that happen. After a long day of travel and working at our event, we woke early the next day and set out for the beach.

In those days she was a bundle of nerves. Every day was filled with new experiences that she had missed during her years in the fog of addiction. On our way to the beach, she said, "I'm afraid."

I asked, "Why are you afraid?"

"Sharks. In the water."

I assured her there would be no sharks—the water would be too shallow. We both laughed.

At the shoreline, Dorris took off her shoes and dug her toes deep into the sugary sand. From that safe spot, we watched the huge waves offshore rumble toward us, getting smaller and smaller, until their foamy edges tickled the damp sand. When I stepped into the shallow water, Dorris tentatively followed me. The power of the waves surprised her.

"I'm nervous that they'll suck me in."

I smiled at her. "Don't worry. The waves are really gentle close to shore."

She looked up, threw her head back, and raised her arms, delighted. "Has this been doing this my whole life?"

"Yes, Dorris, your whole life."

She'd seen the underside of bridges, the inside of a jail cell, and the dirty carpets of crack houses. But she'd never seen the ocean. Her laugh that day, as always, was infectious, and through her eyes I saw the ocean's majesty in a new way.

Dorris Walker is awesome. A delightful woman with big faith. And her singing voice moves me to tears. When I think of her, I smile. I'm so glad you're getting to meet her.

Becca Stevens
Founder and President, Thistle Farms

DORRIS'S STORY

Dorris Walker lost nearly three decades of her life—from her thirties through most of her fifties. She should have been kissing her son and daughter at bedtime, cheering them on at soccer games, dabbing her eyes at graduations, and then enjoying the freedom of an empty-nester. But while she lived through those decades, she was by no means fully alive. Twenty-six years were stolen from her and her family by a devastating crack addiction.

No one would have predicted this.

She was born into a poor but loving home in White House, Tennessee, with two parents who adored her. The child of sharecroppers, she was brought up to share and most of all to give thanks to her Lord. But a tragic misunderstanding ruined her happy childhood.

One day while Dorris played outside, her aunt charged into their yard. Enraged, she believed Dorris's sister was responsible for breaking up her daughter's marriage. She attacked Dorris's mother—her own sister—and then pulled out a gun and shot Dorris's father. Her mother survived, but her dad didn't. The life she'd known for twelve short years died with him.

His absence left her with a consuming ache in her heart. She felt angry, confused, consumed with grief. When a classmate offered her a joint after school one day, and she quickly became addicted.

By eighteen, her father's absence became an all-consuming longing for a man's attention. When a man five years older came along, she married him and had a son and a daughter—outwardly the perfect family. But behind closed doors, her alcoholic husband raged and beat her. Marijuana remained her only comfort.

Finally, she packed up, loaded her children into her car, and drove to White House to stay with her mom. She thought she was free, but she tossed and turned at night, unable to sleep. She began visiting with a childhood friend, smoking weed with her and her husband while Dorris's mom watched her kids at home. One night, Dorris sent her friend out for more marijuana, but she came back with cocaine instead. Another friend cooked it into rocks of crack.

Dorris couldn't cope with her emotional pain sober, and at that moment, crack was her only option. One night, one hit, would turn the thirty-two-year-old mother into a crack addict.

Within days, her life spiraled out of control. She stopped showing up to work and was fired. Without money, her friend ended the invitations to her home. Dorris still found ways to come up with enough money to drive into Nashville to buy drugs.

One day, she asked her brother's friend, a crack user, she asked him for drugs on credit. He agreed to drugs without payment —as long as she had sex with him. Her stomach lurched, but the need for crack was stronger than her repulsion. *Just a few minutes*, she thought, *and I'll get what I need.*

Even though she had no plans to do it again, without a job, turning tricks became an easy way to make money for drugs.

She became a shell of her former self, barely sleeping or eating, walking the streets of Nashville, staying up constantly, chasing the next hit. When she did go home, close to shutting down from drug abuse and sheer exhaustion, her mother cared for her. But Dorris always was out the door again, knowing that in White House, her mother continued to pray, begging God to deliver her.

Drugs gripped her so strongly that she kept turning tricks even after a john tortured her and threatened to kill her. She couldn't go to the police. No one would believe her, and they might arrest her. Getting in a stranger's car was scary, but not having money to buy crack was worse.

When she didn't feel like turning tricks, she wrote bad checks to buy food or new tea-length dresses. But the bad checks caught up with her. Arrested for check fraud, she served nine months at the Tennessee Prison for Women.

Those nine months should have been life-changing. She was clean and completely sober for the first time in years. Instead, the moment she walked out of the prison, she set out to find a hit. She believed just a little crack could help her lose the hundred pounds she'd gained in prison. But one hit reset her addiction.

Years passed in much the same way. Even after stays a couple of rehabs, she went right back to the nearest crack house. For twenty-six years, she feared she would die as an addict, a hooker, a screwed-up person who couldn't even make it to her own son's high school graduation.

The day Dorris was arrested again and hauled to the Davison County Jail seemed like a typical day for a crack addict. In the common room, she was startled to see her old friend Regina, who used to smoke crack with her on the streets. When she disappeared, Dorris thought she was probably dead, but here she was, a volunteer at the prison. Regina was clean.

She told Dorris about a two-year program run by Thistle Farms that healed her addiction and took her off the streets. For the first time, Dorris dared hope there was a way out after all. But it took another rock-bottom moment for her to finally call. When she learned she'd have to wait weeks, even months. she thought her heart might break. But then a miracle happened. Regina called with news that would change Dorris' life—there was room for her after all.

On November 9, 2009, Dorris stepped into her new life at Thistle Farms. She could hardly believe it. The place was nothing like any prison, rehab, or halfway house she'd associated with recovery. She dove into therapy, counseling, new relationships with other women who'd walked the streets of addiction before her. They put her to work in their product production facility. She was on a new path.

But then, tragedy struck. Her beloved mother, who had cared for her children and prayed for her through her addiction, had a stroke the day before Dorris' birthday, and deep depression settled over her. Her new life of promise suddenly felt dark and hopeless. Yet, God still protected her, and she found the strength keep walking toward her new life

Faith had always been part of Dorris's life, but as she began to read the devotional book *Jesus Calling*, she realized she'd never asked God to be the Lord of her life or to deliver her from her wasted years. In the quiet of her bedroom, she surrendered herself to the Lord. Looking back, she knows Jesus is the reason she's over a decade clean today.

Dorris began working at Thistle Farms's job-training program. Her heart nearly burst with pride when she received her first paycheck. Eventually, she received a promotion to manage the packing department.

Dorris's daughter and grandchildren were in the crowd cheering when she walked across a stage in 2011 and received her certificate of completion. During her moment of triumph, she looked at her daughter and knew she'd never go back to the streets.

Thistle Farms promoted her to director of events, a position that allowed her to travel around the country sharing her story. She signed a lease for her own apartment, and after a few years, her son, who'd refused to come visit after she got clean, finally showed up for dinner and was inseparable from her after that.

Years went by. Dorris was still clean. Still working at Thistle Farms. Still spreading her story far and wide. She loved her life and felt guilty asking for more. But a deep longing still nagged at her soul. More than anything, she wanted a husband. She wanted a man to share his life with her, who could look beyond her past. At times, it seemed too tall an order even for God.

Then, James Taylor walked into her church, a man she'd known since they were kids. She called him Jaybird back then. He was a widower now, with a gentle spirit and a smile that made her weak in the knees. For the first time in decades, she found herself in a relationship with no price, no dollars exchanged. She trusted James. She wasn't afraid. So when he knelt down before her with a ring in a velvet box, she squealed as she shouted, "Yes!"

Today, Dorris can hardly believe she gets to call this life her own. It isn't perfect. Money is tight, and she has a few more aches and pains than she used to. But her worst day today is leaps and bounds better than her best day on the street. A look back proves to her that hope is *always* real. Hope for anyone battling addiction. Hope for anyone who calls on the Lord. Hope for anyone who dreams of a better life. Dorris is living proof.

Note: All references to Magdalene throughout the book are to what is known today as Thistle Farms Residential. When Dorris was first introduced to Thistle Farms, the residential home was called Magdalene.

PROLOGUE

woke up at Mama's home in White House, Tennessee, with that old, gnawing feeling in my stomach. All night I'd dreamed I was back on the streets of Nashville smoking crack. Now, stone-cold sober, one thought raced through my mind.

"I gotta get another hit."

I knew my mama hoped I'd decide to stay. Maybe I wouldn't go back. Maybe I wouldn't sell my body anymore. Maybe I wouldn't stay stoned out of my mind. But I couldn't do it. This is who I am. I don't deserve no better. After twenty-six years on the street, I felt it was too late to change.

I shoved every dress I owned into the little cloth bag on my bed. "I gotta get out of here."

Even the scent of bacon and eggs wafting into my room couldn't convince me to stay another second. I was stone-cold sober and needed a hit, and fast.

I'd stayed at my mama's for ten days. She asked me to come home and sing in her church choir's anniversary celebration. I'd kept my promise. She couldn't make me stay any longer. I just needed to get a ride back to Nashville.

I picked up the phone and dialed every number I knew by memory. Usually, finding a ride was easy, because everybody on the street is always looking to make a few extra bucks, but nobody bit. I was so busy dialing I barely noticed the deep, rhythmic humming coming from the next room. My mom didn't sing the words, but I immediately recognized the old African American spiritual I'd heard my whole life.

Oooooh, Lord, I want you to help me.

"Lord, don't you let my baby go back out there!" I heard her scream before she went back to humming.

I didn't even flinch. *Mama's praying again.* After all the years she'd prayed, it wasn't enough to sway me now. I was going back to the streets.

"Dorris, come in and eat!" Mama yelled from the kitchen.

I ignored her, still waiting for somebody to pick up the phone. By now, panic was rising. *Why ain't somebody coming?*

"Dorris." She peeked through the curtain that served as a bedroom door. Her voice was soothing, like she was waking me up. But when she saw me next to the bed, with the bulging cloth bag beside me, her face changed.

"What are you doing?" She already knew the answer.

"I'm getting ready to go, Mama. I did what you asked me to do."

Tears welled in her big brown eyes. I didn't want to watch them roll down her wrinkled face, so I turned my back to her.

"You doing what?" Her voice quivered and cracked the way it did when she cried.

"I just got something to do. I'm going back."

"You don't have anything to do. Where are you going?"

I turned. Her cheeks were wet with tears. If I'd had any sense, I would have stopped and promised to stay. But I didn't have any sense. My brain was too clouded with drugs to see the truth.

CHAPTER 1

Untarnished Hope

I was born on a Sunday morning, January 22, 1956. My father and mother, Forrest Ulysses Utley and Lockey Dee Williams Utley, were poor in the eyes of those who measure success by money. Yet they had a wealth of love and faith. Humble believers in God, they served and loved people in our community, believed the Good Book, and tried to do what it said.

My parents were sharecroppers in rural Tennessee, where they farmed and raised livestock for the landowners—tobacco, chickens, cows, and other farm animals—in exchange for a place to live and a credit line at the nearby grocery that was paid off at the end of the year. It was a hard life, working long hours and raising five kids. I am the youngest; then Joe, James, and Lansford, my older brothers; and one sister, Portia.

We lacked money, but not love and faith. As poor as we were, Mama always fed the field hands who worked alongside my dad at harvest time before she fed us kids. I remember complaining, "Why do they get to eat first? I'm hungry!" But she insisted we treat every stranger as a possible angel.

"Do unto others as you would have them do unto you," she'd remind me. "They are our guests and we must always make them feel welcomed. Remember what the Bible says, 'Do not neglect to show hospitality to strangers, for some have entertained angels unaware.'"

Most folks dreaded the rain, but I loved it. While my parents scrambled to find buckets to catch the drips in the house, I went to bed thinking, *Tomorrow I'll be able to make lots and lots of mud pies!* The next morning, when I made mud pies, I felt really creative—I used *grass* to substitute for cake sprinkles. I loved humming the way Mama did when she baked biscuits, cakes, and pies.

The bulk of my toys and childhood games were 99 percent creativity and imagination. I loved Shirley Temple, so I took twine string that fell from Daddy's wagons and tractors, and wound it around the post of the front porch. After a rain, I imagined that those twine curls were the perfect long blonde locks of hair like Doris Day and Shirley Temple, even though it was hard to tell on a black-and-white TV.

I also loved Doris Day's singing. When I was alone, I pretended a hairbrush was a microphone and strutted in front of the mirror, pretending to be her while I sang my heart out. I knew I'd grow up and shake this little town to become a singer or movie star.

As far back as I remember, I loved music. My dad, a tall, lanky man, sang tenor in the church choir, and filled our home with music morning, noon, and night. I was the kid in our family who could carry a tune, so as soon as I could talk in sentences, Daddy had me singing with him.

I was happy and healthy and full of hope. Some was childlike, like "I hope I don't forget to say grace before eating so there will be enough food to go around." Or, "I hope Mama has enough to eat after we finish."

We lived a simple but joyous lifestyle. I never thought of my family as poor because of the hope the seven of us shared and the rituals of daily prayers.

I believed the Lord would make a way *somehow*. If I knew nothing else, I knew that *hope always kept our family going*. For instance, we hoped for our own home year after year and never gave up.

Finally, by the end of 1968, when I was twelve, my parents had saved enough money to move off the farm and into their own home. We had done without meals enough so that we would have our own food for well over twenty years.

When my parents told us we were moving to our own place, I nearly jumped up and down with excitement. They both had gotten what we called "public jobs" at a cabinet company, and finally we had enough money to build a new house. We left the farm and became homeowners.

They were so proud and we were all smiles—like we'd reached our Promised Land of milk and honey. In the evenings, after a long day at work, Dad would continue to clear off the thickets and thistles on our property.

My parents taught and instilled faith-filled family values. I learned over the next decades how important a lifestyle full of hope would become in my life.

Many educational sources have documented the importance of the early family environment to form a person's life. The Bible agrees. Proverbs 22:6 says, "Train up a child in the way that he should go; when he is old he will not depart from it."

I was raised going to church, believing in who God is, and the love He has for all His creation. These teachings, even when I didn't follow them over the next thirty years or so, still echoed in my heart and mind:

- Believe in God, believe in Jesus, and believe in the power of prayer.

- Live with honesty and integrity. Be honest; don't change who you are. Be a person of integrity and always keep your word—our word is all we have.

- Share and take turns. Do unto others as you would have them do unto you.

- Live in hope. God always keeps His promises, and we are never beyond His love and His ability to care for His children.

- Respect others. Treat a stranger as God would want you to; that person could be an angel unaware.

- Be kind. Kindness is power.

- Have gratitude. Do not grumble, but be grateful for what you have. Things could always get worse.

- Consider others. Think about how others feel when you are making decisions.

- Learn to forgive. If I can forgive others, God will forgive me.

What values from your past set the right foundation for your life? Perhaps you didn't have positive principles instilled from birth like I did. My early family and church teaching didn't keep me and those

I loved safe from tragedy. Still, the hope in my heart, while often deep underground, never fully left me. I believe that's why I am still here today.

Some lessons from my early life were more difficult to live out after my childhood. Like forgiving someone who has intentionally harmed me without a reason. The Bible says, "If you forgive other people when they sin against you, your heavenly Father will also forgive you, but if you do not forgive others their sins, your Father will not forgive your sins" (Matthew 6:14–15, NIV). That would soon be particularly hard in my family.

I struggled like many people to remain joyful and hopeful through the storms of life. The Bible says, "Consider it pure joy, my brothers and sisters, whenever you face trials of many kinds, because you know that the testing of your faith produces perseverance" (James 1:2–3, NIV). My trials and storms made holding on nearly impossible—but not completely.

I also learned hard things at twelve—what it meant to be truly afraid. I'd define fear as an unpleasant emotion caused by the belief that someone or something is dangerous, likely to cause pain, or a threat. That set me on a path for decades that made trusting others and myself—even God—increasingly hard.

I was taught the right values. You may have been too. I was given a strong foundation for my life. Even in hard situations, I was assured countless times that the Lord would make a way. I was told nothing is too hard for God. So, at twelve, I thought life would be easy. I was wrong, but God's promises would prove to be true.

No matter what happened in our past, we need to look back, not to wallow in sorrow or pain at the hard times but to recall where we came from. We should reflect on all God did for us, how He never left us alone. He constantly reminded the Israelites to remember what He had done so they could see His long record of faithfulness. Then they could face the path ahead of them.

This looking back helps you gain a better understanding of how God has worked in people and situations. And that insight leads to success. God's promise "I will never leave you nor forsake you" is found in multiple books of the Bible, in both the Old and New Testaments. This promise assures us of His unwavering presence and encourages us to lean on Him in faith and spirit.

While your early teaching set a foundation for how you handle the present and the future, it's never too late to learn or relearn the right values. I hope my story will help you take a purposeful look at your life—the good and the painful circumstances—and learn that God will be with you on the journey yet to come.

At twelve years old, I assumed life would be perfect. We'd never be hungry, lonely, or poor. I thought I'd arrived the day we moved in to our new house. It was only three bedrooms, but to me it might as well have been a palace.

The dream fulfilled didn't last a month.

CHAPTER 2

Hope Crushed

On Monday, May 6, 1968, birds chirped, the sun shone, and we enjoyed our new house. All was well in my world.

My two oldest brothers were married and living on their own. My sister Portia, a college sophomore, was home for a semester living with my parents, my eighteen-months-older brother Lansford, who was thirteen, and me.

We had other family nearby. Our cousin Emma lived down the street with her husband and five children. Her mother, Aunt Isabelle, was Mama's younger sister. She often told me I was beautiful, and I thought I was her favorite niece.

Portia needed a job to help with expenses at home and for college, so she and Emma, a grade-school dropout, went job hunting. Although my sister was much more qualified, they helped each other look for employment. Emma had the use of their family car and Portia needed rides.

Earlier that week, they applied for the same temporary job, which Portia got. Emma seemed to take it in stride and offered to let

Portia ride to work with her husband, Jimmy, until the temporary job ended. So my sister and Jimmy carpooled from Monday, May 6 through Thursday, May 9.

At the end of that fourth day, Jimmy went home, packed his clothes, and told his wife and five kids he was leaving—for good, with no explanation.

Emma called her mother, crying, claiming without reason or proof that Portia had stolen her husband in the four days they rode to work together. The accusations infuriated Isabelle, who grew enraged over lies she never bothered to verify.

The next afternoon Aunt Isabelle marched into our yard, yelling. I was playing in the front yard as she charged onto our driveway, her eyes blazing with rage. She screamed and carried on, demanding to see my sister.

"Portia! Come out here! Portia!"

I noticed the huge stick she held and thought she'd come to help us battle the weeds.

Little did I know she was armed to kill.

She continued to shout, "Portia, come out here!"

Mama and Daddy hurried outside and invited her to come inside, unable to figure out why she was so upset.

With fire in her eyes, Isabelle cursed and shouted, "Where's Portia? She broke up my daughter's marriage!"

Isabella had worked herself into pure rage over a mere rumor.

Although I was scared, I thought, *I can calm her down. I'm her favorite niece.* So, I waved to her. "Hi, Aunt Isabelle."

She glared at me like she had never seen me before.

No one else noticed the clublike stick—until she whacked my mom—her own sister—over the head, splitting her skull. I heard a loud, horrible sound, like somebody had cracked open a ripe watermelon.

Blood gushed everywhere. Mama fell, but remained conscious. Then I heard another unfamiliar sound—my mom moaning in pain and anguish.

In an instant Daddy rushed to Isabelle, snatched the stick, and threw it on the ground. I didn't see the gun until I heard a loud pop. She'd shot him in the side.

The sound was deafening. Time slowed.

I still remember my blood-curdling scream as my dad slumped to the ground.

"Aaaaaaaaaaahhhhhhhh!!!

As I ran toward him, he fell, which resulted in my leg being partially trapped underneath my dying father. The next few minutes were a blur. I got out from under him and saw and felt warm blood from his side and on the tips of my shoes. The air was filled with my mom's painful groans and my sobs.

My aunt ran away through the back field. Somebody called for an ambulance. Forty-five minutes passed before the emergency workers showed up, but by then Daddy was long dead. Mama still needed urgent attention.

At some point, Portia came into the room. Overwhelmed by the horror, with me covered in blood, we ran into my parents' room seeking safety from the situation. We opened the chifforobe and took out Daddy's suit and held it. His scent provided a small comfort to my heart, because everything around me was chaos.

Our neighbor, Mr. Robert Taylor, the first to arrive, told my brother Lansford, "You gotta step up, son. You're the man of the house now."

Something about his solemn statement drove my loss home to me. I knew life would never be the same.

When my father died, the life I'd known for twelve years died with him.

Fifty years have come and gone, but I remember that day like it was yesterday. I'll never forget, no matter how hard I try.

Those events ruined the hope I'd taken for granted for twelve years.

Looking back, I don't know if the weight of my dad's body or the weight of life without him crushed me, and what I'd always believed. When I got up from the ground, nothing was ever the same.

Mama's injuries affected me too. Although she survived, she was too damaged to attend Daddy's funeral. Somebody took Polaroids of the coffin to show her and help her find closure. I didn't need a picture. The sight of Daddy lying lifeless in that box was forever burned in my brain. Day after day, I tried to stop that image from popping up in my mind, to stop seeing him reeling back, blood spurting from his body as the bullet hit. I desperately wanted the whole incident to be a dream, but that constant nightmare was my reality.

From the day she got home from the hospital, Mama was a different person—stern, strict, and ready to pounce. She wouldn't let me out of her sight for any activities. I wasn't allowed to do things my friends got permission for without their parents thinking twice. Even years later, I was only allowed to attend my senior prom if I took my brother as my date. Needless to say, I missed the dance.

Looking back, I understand she feared losing one of us too. But back then, I hated the feeling of constantly living under somebody's thumb.

In reality, I lost both parents who raised me with unbridled love, joy, and hope.

The days of singing in front of the bathroom mirror, of dancing around, of feeling any kind of happiness ended. Sadness clung like an unwanted second skin, sucking the life out of my heart and soul.

My comforting sense of family died with Daddy—I no longer knew what family meant. The aunt I thought adored me, killed my father and injured my mother. Mama changed from the carefree pillar of faith I knew, which snatched away my hope-filled childhood. I began to live in denial. That traumatic day left me with a huge emotional hole in my soul I tried desperately to fill with anything I could find.

So 'one day when a boy named Johnny' offered me a joint, I took it without a pause. As I inhaled the smoke, my brain went numb. For the first time since Daddy died, my mind was free of the image of his blood spilling on the ground. I wasn't sad. I wasn't angry. I didn't feel anything at all. And I wanted more.

From then on, marijuana became my crutch; smoking a daily routine. Emotional pain returned when the high faded, but marijuana provided a short relief.

I was addicted at thirteen.

My hope was crushed at twelve when I watched and felt my dad take his last breath.

My hope was crushed when Mama became a different person, and I lost the security of two loving parents.

My hope was crushed when I turned to drugs to escape.

My hope was crushed when I ran away later and left my own children because I couldn't cope with the life I tried to build after that tragic day.

My hope was crushed in many ways and many times in the first decades of my life.

Even in my older years, I have often felt that time has run out and my dreams and hopes of becoming an author and speaker might be lost.

Yet along the way I also discovered I'm not alone, that others experience hope-crushing circumstances in life too. They threaten to not only diminish our dreams but eliminate them.

Transitions in Life

We can feel our hopes dash as we age, and experience the physical and mental changes in our lives. During transitional times in our adult lives, we may assess our situation, how we fit into our community, what goals we've met, and find ourselves lacking. Faith may fade as we realize how many of our expectations and even assumptions haven't turned out the way we dreamed.

During these times we have to deal with difficult adjustments. Knowing that changes are inevitable, we need to lean on God's strength to accept circumstances with courage to move through times of crisis without losing hope.

Changing Friendship

As social beings, we seek love and friendship, key elements of an overall healthy life. We simply cannot do without friends because we aren't made to survive alone. We seek and keep friends to help us grow. So a shift in friendship can be difficult because, sometimes we need to let go of people. Other times we need to engage with new faces while releasing people we loved, but need to leave behind. This can be challenging.

People come and go—an inevitable truth about life. We may recall the oft-repeated internet comment and nod in agreement:

"Those who want to stay in your life will find ways to do so." Don't be afraid to welcome new friends or let go of old ones.

Breakups

A broken dating relationship shatters the heart. When love changes to disappointment or abuse, the situation requires strength and wisdom. Instead of letting loss rip away hope, believe that separation and a fresh start will lead to something new and good. Keep your mind busy doing something productive, and know that love can happen again. With healthy physical, emotional, and spiritual practices, pain will subside. Use the season of adjustment to motivate yourself toward positive change.

Failures

Failures affect us in many ways. When we don't make our personal or work goals, we may experience a sense of worthlessness and a cloud of negativity. These keep us down emotionally and mentally and affect our thinking. They are hard to swallow. However, we can choose to read stories of people who succeeded after failures, and discover how important patience and perseverance are to the process of recovering. The best thing to do during these times is to find inspiration and push through.

Divorce

Marriage takes consistent effort to function well. We've all witnessed or had a failed marriage that led to divorce, and know the outcome is difficult for the whole family—a terrible experience.

If you've lost hope after a divorce, remember that it isn't the end but a fresh beginning. This new chapter of your life can open up doors for positive changes. Begin by forgiving and releasing bitterness. Work to make the new type of family you now have the best possible. The right attitude toward life after divorce infuses you with hope.

Losing a Job

Losing a job can be devastating and lead to hunger or even homelessness. I know how hard it is to spend days with an empty stomach.

So what do you do?

Fight the urge to give up and try to find another job. Believe that God will provide and give you strength and perseverance. Seek whatever help is available. Hold on and take action, knowing that life can get better.

Accidents and Disease

Accidents happen and sickness occurs, despite our precautions. We can keep a positive mindset, moving forward with caution while making healthy choices. Recovering from severe injuries serves up long-term, even permanent challenges. To live with unexpected disabilities from disease or injury means major physical, social, career, and emotional adjustments.

Again, maintaining the right attitude energizes you to pursue solutions. To fight depression, concentrate on taking small steps each day. The long journey of recovery can be less stressful by engaging with other people who support a positive outlook. Spend time with loved ones and friends. Take up new activities that your new restrictions don't prevent. For example, some people with cancer have written great novels from their hospital beds.

Death of a Loved One

Death, the ultimate finality, can come to anyone at any time. The sorrow that follows is always tough. Living without loved ones is one of the worst challenges in life.

The stages of grief—denial, anger, depression, bargaining and acceptance—don't occur in the same order or frequency for everyone. Some stages repeat or overlap. Some of us take much longer to arrive at acceptance. Some respond in ways others don't understand. All grief can lead to hopelessness.

Yet death demands grief, so grieving well takes us to the place where we best honor our lost loved ones with acceptance and press ahead with the business of living. Re-engaging restores hope.

* * * * *

While these circumstances and others can hurt us, I felt shame when I realized I had quit believing. I was taught to never give up because the Lord will always make a way. As a Christians, we are never alone. Christ Jesus is our hope in our every circumstance.

When we feel crushed, and our dreams are shattered, never to be fulfilled, we sometimes can't see beyond our pain to grasp God. In these times we struggle to believe there will ever be a better day.

Initially, I failed at following all the training I received as a child. As a believer in Christ, I had been taught we can always move forward and trust the Lord to make a way.

Losing my father shouldn't have made me turn away from the truths that had created a loving, faith-filled foundation for me. I let the tragedy take away all my hope and self-respect. Despair, depression, and drugs rushed into the vacuum. Whenever we leave room for darkness, the enemy comes in like a flood with false hope and addiction.

My addiction quickly progressed. By the time I was an adult, my full-blown cocaine dependence took me to the streets of Nashville, where I led a dark lifestyle for a couple of decades.

My life was no longer worth living.

You don't have to lose decades like I did. Instead, draw on the truth of the Bible and faith in Christ. God loves you and will never give up on you. His hope is always alive. In his last moments on earth, my father protected me with his physical body. Later, the words of hope and faith he taught me resurfaced to sustain and protect me. During my dark decades without hope, his words never fully left me. And they proved true when I finally placed myself in the hands of my Daddy's father, our heavenly Father.

CHAPTER 3

False Hope

By the time I turned eighteen, I felt desperate to get out of Mama's house and away from her rules. I resented the way she fussed at me as if everybody in White House watched my every move. She believed our family had suffered the ultimate disgrace when my aunt killed my dad, which drove her to prove we were better than that.

"We gotta live it down," she told me—more times than I could count.

I guess that's why I rushed into marriage with the first guy who paid attention to me. Clifford, five years older, brought home a steady paycheck working for the railroad, and wore bibbed overalls like Daddy had. Sometimes, in the right light, he even looked a little like Daddy. After only six months of dating, he looked into my eyes and said, "Let's get married."

"Okay," I said.

I expected marriage to restore my crushed hope after Daddy's death. I was too young and inexperienced to realize I couldn't replace my missing father with a husband.

Mama didn't like him from the start because she noted all the red flags I chose to ignore—the dents in his car fender he tried to explain away, the way he staggered into her house, the stench of beer that wafted off his body.

"Don't do it, Dorris," she said. "I know his mother and father. His dad used to beat up his mom. A boy who grows up watching that might do the same thing."

I rolled my eyes. *Yeah, right.*

She never let me do anything, so why should getting married be any different? I ignored every warning she gave me when I walked down the aisle and said, "I do."

We'd barely returned from our honeymoon when I learned not to cross my husband when he'd had too much to drink—which was most days. I wore long sleeves to cover the bruises, and made excuses for the scratch on my face or the dark purple circle around my eye. Still, I stayed. Maybe I feared I'd never find anybody else. Maybe I didn't want to admit that my mom was right. Maybe I thought giving up would cost me even my shaky, false hope. In any case, I stayed.

I hoped the abuse would stop when I gave my husband a daughter, and then a son, but it didn't. Thankfully, he never hurt them, but only targeted me with his violent rages when he was drunk.

I poured myself into my kids. Their chubby little cheeks and sweet hugs and kisses made my life worth living, and reminded me they were worth fighting for. Those two kept my fragile thread of hope alive. Even if I couldn't choose a good husband, I could be a good mom.

I kept up appearances the best I could—I didn't want anyone to know what happened behind closed doors. The neighbors thought we had the perfect family. I shuttled the kids around every night to karate and baton twirling practice. I hosted all the neighborhood kids for sleepovers. I had become my own mother, trying to live down my disgrace.

When we compare ourselves to others, we believe that if we could just attain what they have, we'll be successful and happy. What we don't know is how many people live a different life behind closed doors like I did.

While I kept up the façade, I lived in constant fear of another beating, another bruise to cover up, and another lie to Mama concealing the daily terror I faced.

The only way I survived was to keep myself numb. Every morning, when my alarm went off, I smoked a joint before I woke up the kids. After I dropped the kids at school, I smoked another. Then another on my lunch break during my job at Whirlpool. And another when I got home. The more I smoked, the more I needed it.

Yet marijuana failed to make my abusive marriage bearable. After nine years, I couldn't take it anymore. When my husband wasn't home, I packed up our bags, loaded the car, and took my kids to the safety of my mother's place back in White House.

I had failed. Once again, my brittle hope shattered. Going home felt like quitting. I had failed at creating a family. Even Mama's controlling ways were better than facing my abusive husband every day.

Unfortunately, that wasn't the only time in my life I tried to create my own hope.

After my childhood trauma, Mama said, "Live it down. Hold your head high. Dress well. Smile. Don't worry. Be happy."

So I put on a mask of false hope, afraid no one would like me if I looked or acted as though something was wrong or I had a problem.

I married based on false hope. I pretended to be a supermom behind a fake mask I wore for the world. Yet deep inside I knew I couldn't keep living just relying on fabricated hope.

While I lived on the streets of Nashville, I wore that same mask. When I dressed up and spoke well, even in the worst, most fearful situations, I thought I would feel better about myself and the choices I was making. I believed if I looked and talked properly, I could avoid mental and emotional injury. That hope was false—a lie. I was eaten alive.

I put on a brave face when someone pointed a gun at my head, and every time I marched into a jail cell. *If I don't look defeated, scared, and hopeless, then maybe I won't be.* False hope. A mask.

During my first rehab I repeated that pattern. I liked the appearance of getting help. I entered thinking that if I just hoped enough, it would work. I would get my life back. But I never truly believed I was worth what it would take to successfully overcome my addictions. I repeated that pattern at more than one rehab.

We wear our masks and say "I'm fine" when we aren't. We may think saying it will make it so, and our circumstances will change. We don't want others to see past our mask to our deep pain, shame, and needs. If so, they may discover our true selves—filled with uncertainty, pain, disappointment, and fear. Then they may try to control us like Mama did, or hurt us, like my husband. So we wear masks as flimsy protection. We build walls to keep others out, and alienate people who might help us.

Why do we lean on lies, showing a brave face or manipulating our situations to make us feel better? It's all temporary. When we are fearful, filled with self-loathing, or unable to face the reality of our circumstances, we frantically grasp for anything to hold on to. But nothing and no one can sustain our hope except the one who created us and knows us better than we know ourselves.

I was raised with real hope, which comes from knowing the love of our heavenly Father, a love like no other. Still, the enemy lured me away to seek a solution to my difficulties by creating my own hope. That Band-Aid fell apart quickly, whenever I tried to fix things myself. When I looked for ways to appear okay, I settled for short-lived good feelings.

We know everything that shines or glitters is not gold. The shimmering lie "If you come with me, I will take care of you," often sounded believable, but wasn't. Trusting the wrong people brought me harm and pain, so I learned to wear false hope like a glove. I faked my appearance to the world.

Why do we care what others think of us? Unfortunately, we learn early to seek the company and acceptance of the "cool kids." We believe we need to be around the popular people, when the truth is, we need to be true to who God created us to be. When we hope in the wrong things or put our faith in our appearance or a particular crowd, we risk our true calling from God.

"If I stay in this job, which doesn't suit me, and pay my bills, all will be well."

"If I can make friends with so-and-so, I'll have more attention, more success, more money."

"If I dress trendy and go to the right places, I'll find my one true love."

But when we look to the wrong things for our self-worth and hope, we miss out on what God has in store for us, which is exceedingly and abundantly more than we could ever think to ask for (see Ephesians 3:20).

We sometimes put our faith in untrustworthy people, situations, and comfort zones instead of in God. Trusting people may sound good, even easy, but God requires us to place our hope in things unseen. We must commit ourselves to believing and reading the Word of God, which will transform our minds.

Addiction, abuse, and trauma layered me inside with scars that made me forget my worth. I covered the pain up with an image, a fake look to hide my shame, which somehow became true.

Now that I've regained my self-worth, my insides match my outsides. That's the definition of integrity—pure freedom.

If you cover who you really are with an image, consider doing what I did. Get honest with someone about where you've been. Take that first step to freedom. For me, it made all the difference.

The Bible reminds us that through Christ "you believe in God, who raised him from the dead and glorified him, and so your faith and hope are in God" (1 Peter 1:21, NIV). We can't base our hope on the temporary circumstances of life that constantly change but rather in God, who never waivers. Thankfully, He's also a God who will never leave us, and who often gives us new glimpses of His love and hope if we'll open our eyes to see.

CHAPTER 4

Glimmers of Hope

My father's murder cost my mother her husband and her sister, who went to prison. Even though Mama refused to press charges, the state couldn't let Aunt Isabella get away with murder.

Despite Mama's broken heart, she remained a strong woman of faith. Proud of the life she'd built with her beloved husband, she refused to fall apart. She had three kids to raise, and she still had her faith.

She decided the shame of the tragedy wouldn't define our family. She and my father believed their children should get a good education and make something of themselves. Mama prioritized dressing nicely and looking respectable. Even during the tough early days, she made sure we looked good. After Daddy died, none of that changed. She did all she could to lift us up and make our lives better. She became more controlling, yes, but to keep us safe, steadfastly moving all of us forward. Her courage and strength—when I was falling apart—demonstrated her strong hold on God's hope.

In the small moments when I saw Mama as positive, not controlling, I glimpsed God's love. So while I fed my addiction to marijuana every day and lived in despair, time with Mama showed bits of the hope I'd known before. Sometimes that kept me going and prevented me from bottoming out.

Unfortunately, these small signs weren't enough to keep me from the path of self-destruction. For decades I turned away from the God I knew as a child. When I became a full-blown crack-cocaine addict, and lived on the Nashville streets, my overwhelming shame made me avoid my family. Whenever I returned to her house, I never stayed long. During those times, even though I wanted no part of her efforts to fix me, God used her to bring me a small measure of self-respect—symbolized by my tea-length dresses.

Mama worked at Castner-Knott department store for most of the years I lived on the streets. She never gave up hope that I'd come back and, and "quit running with those folk." She never specified who she didn't want me with. That's how she bolstered her belief I wasn't too far gone. Maybe her hope kept my diminished hope going.

As an act of faith on my behalf, she bought clothes for me using her discount at that department store. I had no real income, so every now and again, when I got as miserable as I could, I'd give up and go back to her house. I'd always find nice dresses in the closet, ready and right for church. She'd throw away the nasty clothes I'd worn for days on end; the stench of smoke and sour body odor couldn't be washed out. Mama never allowed her family to dress poorly to prevent people frowning at us or thinking she did a bad job. So she gave me dresses, which I wore when I went back to Nashville to find my next high.

My Sunday dresses carried a ray of hope back to Nashville—beautiful glimmers of a better life. While I lived on the streets, folks thought I looked churchy. They called me Old School. A crazy thing to call a woman addicted to drugs and selling her body for wadded up cash, but in fact, I appeared to be headed to church, even if I never went.

Dressing differently from other addicts or women in the Nashville alleyways may have been my subconscious way of affirming my life had more value than it appeared at the time. Looking back, I believe God used Mama—and her Castner-Knott employee discount—to keep me from giving up completely.

But Mama wasn't the only place I could see God. He never left me even though I didn't think I deserved His attention. When I looked—often in hindsight—I saw His touch of light and hope in lots of places.

I didn't often have a place to stay, but God brought people here and there who treated me well and befriended me. An older man who mowed lawns for a living, let me hang out with him in his apartment. He was kind to me. He'd been through addiction himself, and knew the havoc drugs wreak on your life. But he never condemned me; he always welcomed me. "You're a good girl, Dorris," he used to tell me. The memory of his simple words went a long way on difficult days.

I even found rays of hope in the middle of rape. How? Because I lived through every single rape. I didn't die. I lived.

I found glimpses of hope behind bars, in a place designed to trap, defeat, and dehumanize me. For a full year while in a small jail in Gallatin, Tennessee, I never saw daylight. But church members came in to teach Bible study and tell us of the goodness of the Lord—spiritual light breaking through the darkness. These moments sustained me a day at a time and kept me waiting for the Lord to restore me.

When I completed rehab and was clean, and God was restoring my relationships, He often reminded me of His presence with me on my darkest nights.

After I became engaged to my current husband, I was on goal to lose weight, yet I craved food more than ever. One evening I told James, "I want to go get a doughnut. Let's go to Krispy Kreme."

Being such an agreeable man, he simply smiled and said, "Okay."

As we left the house, just a few doors down from the place where all my trauma began, we went down the hill toward the little town of Millersville toward the interstate and Krispy Kreme. As we passed a certain mountainous area and a dirt lane off to the side, suddenly I heard this kind, passionate voice whisper into my heart, "Do you remember when I saved your life?"

Suddenly memories from that very spot in the road flooded my mind.

At one point in my addiction, I sat in a crack house, tired and sick and longing to go home. I had only $10. I overheard two guys smoking dope and talking about being from Portland, Tennessee, which was near Mama's house.

I'll wait until they run out of money, because addicts always do. Then I'll offer my last dollar to get a ride to White House, where there are clean sheets and hot food.

They took the bait. I was nervous at first, but the closer we got to my road, I felt safer. Suddenly, they pulled into *that lane* with complete darkness around us. They stopped and demanded I get out of the truck, but I refused because I have a phobia about darkness. They tried to force me out, but I kept yelling, "No, I don't want to! I paid you to take me home!" I did *not* pay them to take me to a dead-end road to do God knows what to me.

As one of them reached for the door handle, headlights hit us all in the face. I have never in my life been so happy to see a police car.

This local cop talked to the two men, then walked over to the truck and said, "Ma'am, you must have angels watching over you, because if you had gotten out of the truck, you would never have been seen again. There's a huge hole right here, and they would've done what they wanted and you would be dead."

The officer put me in his patrol car and drove me another three miles to Mama's house, where I found safety, hot food, and clean sheets. On most days on the streets, the police were the last thing I wanted to see because I might end up in jail. This night, God brought the police to save me.

Years later, on a quick drive to Krispy Kreme, God reminded me of His protection so long before. And by the way . . . I got my doughnut.

Where in your life do you need to be reminded of God's presence, of hope in Him? We all can reach a point of hopelessness at any moment, but what we do with it will determine what comes next. I found that those small glimmers—my Mama's dresses, a friend's encouraging words, reminders of how often God saved me from death—kept me from making more permanent destructive choices. I will always be grateful for those little lights of God's love.

Psalm 119:105 (KJV) says that God's Word is a "lamp unto our feet and a light unto our path." His promises are true. He gives us enough light and hope to keep going, to put one foot in front of the other. This happened many times at low points. I didn't always recognize His presence then, but God stayed with me, and sparked the light of hope into my life.

I couldn't have recovered on my own. The people God used to bring me encouragement and kindness may never know how much they offered me light and even helped save my life. We all need that—some days more than others, some people more than others. And we need to keep our eyes, ears, and hearts open to see those flickers of hope when they come our way.

Yet sometimes it's our turn to offer hope to someone who crosses our path—today, tomorrow, next week, or next year. Because we likely won't know when the opportunity will come, the Bible says we should always be "prepared to make a defense to anyone who asks you for a reason for the hope that is in you; yet do it with gentleness and respect" (1 Peter 3:15, ESV).

You might wonder, "How can I help someone that way? I'm barely making it through today as it is." Recall your time in the proverbial ditch and think about how you made it through. Share that knowledge and experience with someone.

Maybe you don't need hope today, but someone in your path does. Every day.

What is a glimmer of hope? You don't have to be a Bible scholar to offer up hope. It can be conveyed through a smile, a thank you, a kind word, a caring gesture, a voice of encouragement. When you see a need, do what you can to meet it, with love and respect. Let the people you help know the love and hope you share comes from our God who is love, and that they can know Him too.

CHAPTER 5

Hidden Hope

My dresses from Mama helped me hide myself from my true situation on the streets. Somehow, being seen in nice clothes and heels diminished my sense of desperation.

My street clothes tended to conceal my life as a prostitute. I avoided the outfits other girls wore—tight tops and shorts up to their butts. I walked the streets in heels and tea-length dresses—my favorite look since childhood. I supplemented Mama's gifts with cheap clothing to elevate my look. Almost every day, I went to Goodwill looking for the kind of material that moved with me when I walked.

I didn't talk like the others either. At least not at first. If someone said something I didn't quite catch, I'd say, "Pardon?" That's the way I'd been raised. If somebody sneezed, I'd say, "Bless you!" Folks in the crack houses and on the streets laughed at me—my polite comments were ridiculed. Drug dealers laughed in derision when I said, "Thank you," for a rock of crack. I sang gospel songs everywhere I went, the ones I sang with my dad. Once or twice, I got free drugs for singing.

I never completely gave up that identity—the look of a lady and the promise of someday returning to church. It was who I was raised to be. I'd lost my way but many days I just wanted to go back. If only I could figure out how. Underneath my lifestyle beat the heart and soul of a girl who loved Jesus, one raised with heavenly hope. My lifestyle shrouded that hope, but it shone just a little when I wore my favorite dresses.

Still, behind my appearance, I lived in chaos. With no home, I moved from house to house, staying with a buddy here or a boyfriend there. For a while I dated the same guy and thought I might marry him. He even gave me an engagement ring. That relationship ended abruptly when I traded my ring for crack.

"You gotta choose," he shouted at me. "It's the drugs or me."

No contest. I never saw him again.

I stayed up for days on end and rarely ate besides an occasional sausage biscuit and honey bun. I immediately spent every cent I made on the next hit. I didn't think about my kids or what they were doing. I rarely visited them. *They'll be all right. I gotta get a hit. Just one more.*

My body took only so much of the abuse, and then I felt my muscles give out. My feet refused to go another step. Sometimes I felt so sick I couldn't move. Then I'd think, *I'm going home to clean sheets.*

I'd turn a trick for a ride back to my mother's house, the only place I could rest, the only place I knew somebody would take care of me. And Mama always did, even when she flat out told me she didn't like the person I'd become. However long I stayed, she fed me home-cooked meals and gave me vitamins. She threw away my stinking clothes and matted-up wig and dressed me in new tea-length dresses and a brand-new wig.

My kids were always over the moon to see me. I didn't realize how much they hoped that I'd stay. Then they wouldn't have to wonder if I'd ever come back, or if I was somewhere dead on the streets. "You gonna be here when I get home from school, Mama?" my son and daughter asked before they left in the morning.

"Yeah, I'll be here," I assured them. But I wasn't. After about a week or so, I itched for another hit. I pulled out my phone list and called up somebody to give me a ride back to Nashville.

On the streets, in addition to the way I dressed, I held some pride, and maybe a little hope, in my heart. Even when I sold myself for money, I had certain standards, things I wouldn't do. I refused to sleep with another woman, although I regularly did with men for drug money. I told myself, "That's a line I refuse to cross. After all, what would Mama think?"

My rationalizing masked the tiny bit of hidden hope that, like a small ember, still smoldered in my soul. Holding on to that low standard kept a spark alive. However, I also told myself, "When Mama dies, all bets are off." She offered my only link to a decent life.

Amazingly, after I finally got clean, my mother died. In God's perfect timing, He took away my desire for drugs and alcohol before her death. That showed His mercy. If Mama had died sooner, who knows how far I'd have gone? I can't imagine.

Addiction poisons the mind and makes devoted mothers forget everything but getting the next high. I know I sound like a monster. I wish with all my heart that I could go back, that I could recover that time with my kids, that I could squeeze them tight and tell them they meant more to me than anything else. Believe me, I'd rather not tell the world what a terrible mother I was for so long. I tell my story because I want everyone to understand the power of drugs. I want them to see how drugs can transform a normal person into a slave of addiction, and make even the most devoted mother forget about her children, numbing the desire for anything but that high.

You don't have to be an addict to hide your hope behind lifestyle choices, even those that may sound healthy. Whatever takes your focus off the most important relationships of life—God and family—ultimately brings destruction. That idol may be fitness or food, drugs or art, work or media. Even children and family can become an idol, where you lose yourself and destroy the very people you want to lift up.

The Bible says our enemy wants "to kill, to steal, and to destroy" our lives (John 10:10, NKJV), and he will try every possible way to take our hope in God away by replacing it with other temptations. But that same verse promises that Jesus came to give us an abundant life—one full of hope. This gift from God is ours as His children, but we have to keep it from being taken over by everything the world offers us for fulfillment. We listen to voices other than God's, which tell us we'll only truly be happy if we follow this trend, give our attention to this activity, that person, or those drugs.

How then can we live our promised abundant life? How do we sustain our authentic hope and reject temporary fixes? They only give us temporary happiness and hide our true hope under other idols. We can only remain true to our core, God-given selves when we follow His instructions for life. The word Bible can be an acronym for: Basic Information Before Leaving Earth. God has given us a road map for life.

Why should we trust God's Word? We remain true to ourselves and to who God created us to be when we believe in Him. To live an abundant, peaceful, joyful life with God as our healer, deliver, and way-maker, all we need is to believe in Him and His truth.

No matter what circumstances steal or hide our true hope when we trust God's promises, *that* hope doesn't lie or die. When we live with faith-filled standards we've grown up with or even when we make bad choices, God is faithful to restore us to a full, shining hope in a future with Him.

Underneath my sins and self-destruction, I knew better. I believe that when you know better, you eventually will do better. Thankfully, I never lost that desire to return to being the woman God created me to be and live a life He wanted for me—my best life.

A familiar saying is "If you don't stand for something, you'll fall for anything." Another way to put that truth is "Those who stand for nothing will fall." When I didn't stand for the right things, I indeed fell—over and over again— but inside, in my deepest spirit, I knew God was still with me.

Another way to regain hope after we've gone astray is to pray continually. I never stopped praying, even in the worst situations. Despite my outward circumstances, I believed in the name of Jesus and the power of His blood.

On the streets, I only looked the part of a nice lady because I dressed the way I did. Now I look the part from the inside out because God saved me from my path of destruction.

CHAPTER 6

Hope Deferred

I'd had enough. I couldn't hide behind my Supermom persona any more. When my first husband's abuse finally became too much, I quit trying to show the world a perfect family. I packed up, loaded my children into my car, and drove to White House to stay with Mama. I knew she would take care of us. I could finally stop pretending. I was finally free, I thought.

Lying in bed at my mom's house, I couldn't sleep. I was used to sleeping next to my husband, feeling the warmth of his body. Accusing thoughts tormented me. *You're a failure. Here you are a grown woman, back in your mom's house with your kids.*

I couldn't sleep, and I couldn't quit marijuana. I was still addicted, not free.

Living back at Mama's, I had the perfect opportunity to restore all the hope I'd lost between my dad's death and my husband's abuse. Instead, I deferred any hope in favor of my addiction, because I thought it alone could make me feel batter.

One day a childhood friend invited me to hang out at her house. I sat on her couch, cried, and smoked a joint while my mother watched my children. This pattern continued night after night at my friend's kitchen table, smoking marijuana with her and her husband. I quit hiding my mess. I poured out my pain and failure. Her house became my refuge, a desperately needed outlet, so I could go home and be strong for my children, whose lives had been turned upside down.

One night, I handed my friend a wad of bills and told her to bring back a bag of weed. A few hours later, she returned.

"I couldn't find any marijuana, but I found this."

My eyes widened when she laid a bag of white powder on the table.

"I don't want that," I protested. I meant it. I didn't want anything stronger.

But the next night, when my friend's uncle cooked the cocaine into crack, I gave in. I couldn't cope with my emotional pain while sober. At that moment, I needed a hit of something, and crack was my only option. I closed my eyes and took a deep breath. When I held out my hand to take the drug, I didn't know I was signing my life away.

I didn't think I got high. Everybody talked about how addictive crack was, but I thought for sure that one hit wouldn't hurt me or keep me coming back.

I went to work at Kmart the next morning, exhausted after staying up all night. As soon as I clocked out, I intended to head back to my mama's house to get some sleep. Out of nowhere I smelled the distinct scent of rubbing alcohol. My nostrils burned and I swore I could taste it. I wrinkled my nose. *What is that?*

I heard a snap, crackle, pop, like someone scrunched up a wad of cellophane inside my skull. I was *still* high. The crack I'd dismissed as ineffective still flooded my system, twisting my thoughts, manipulating my senses.

I don't know what came over me when I got in my car. Before I could understand my decision, I turned my steering wheel and drove to my friend's house instead. *I just need one more hit. One more and I'll be good.*

I didn't know addiction only required one hit. One night and one hit turned this thirty-two-year-old mother into a crack addict.

Within days, life spiraled out of control.

I never realized my life as I knew it hung by such a fragile thread. Kids, job, reputation—all had seemed so permanent. I didn't know everything could disappear so quickly.

First, I lost my job. I stopped showing up after "just one more hit" turned into another, and another. Soon my boss called to say, "Don't come back."

Without a steady paycheck, my bank account plummeted. Then, my friend who introduced me to crack suddenly didn't want me around when I couldn't keep the whole group supplied with drugs.

Finally, I took off for Nashville, where I knew I could find the drugs my body ached for. The fact that my kids were still with my mom and not with me never crossed my mind. *They'll be all right.* All that mattered was the next hit. My empty bank account didn't stop me from writing checks—and that came back to haunt me later.

I told myself I wasn't an addict. I believed I could stop if I wanted to. That's what crack does. Drug thinking resembles wearing double-vision glasses. I saw the world a certain way, not realizing that if I took off the lenses of warped perception, I'd see a completely different picture.

Any chance I had at restoring myself and my children—any hope
I could've reignited to follow God's path—fled, out of sight with that
first crack hit.

Not even my mom could get through to me.

One day she exploded. "Look at yourself. You've lost your head.
You lost your husband. You lost your job. You lost your kids. What's
wrong with you?"

She pleaded with me to come to my senses. She wanted me to
turn back to the Lord and let God redeem my life. I ignored her and
put Him off. Every time she talked to me, I shrugged without emotion. "I ain't hurting nobody but myself." I believed that.

Crack's pull effectively erased the old Dorris. I functioned like a
sleepwalker, living on autopilot.

After years on the streets and many arrests, I ended up in jail
again. This time I encountered Regina. She and I had hung out together at one time, but she had suddenly disappeared.

Because our lives had so little value on the streets, I assumed Regina was no longer in the land of the living. I thought she'd gotten
into the wrong car, gone home with the wrong person, or died from
badly contaminated drugs.

Regina showed up at the jail that day, but not as an inmate.

"Dorris, guess what!" she bellowed across the room.

"What?"

She shouted, "I got my life back!"

"How did you do that?"

"I found this program called Magdalene—"

I cut her off and threw up my hands in protest. "Oh no, I can't
do that. I've tried to get clean before, but the halfway houses charge
a $140 a week." In those days the only way I knew how to make money

was the only way I knew how to make money. I made eye gestures so Regina understood.

She smiled. "Don't worry about the cost. This program is free for two whole years. You pay nothing, and they even give you a small stipend."

As she beamed and glowed, my heart skipped a beat, excited that there might be a way out, a way to become normal again. But at the words "two years," I dropped my head and muttered. "I can't. I've tried sooooo many times before to get clean."

My outcome at every rehab was failure. I'd enter a thirty-day program, but come out the same way I went in—craving drugs—or unable to continue payment.

Regina was actually clean! Happy, but sad, I suppressed my skepticism when her face lit up like never before. She'd come back to the jail, where she'd been an inmate, to bring comfort and hope for those of us who lived as though the only way to go was down.

Even though she offered me a doorway to hope, I wouldn't walk through. Fear taunted me. *You've tried and failed. This won't be any different. Face it. You're stuck in this life. And look at yourself. You're going to jail again.* The voices of defeat in my head convinced me to put off another chance at restoration.

Through the years God offered me many opportunities to get out of drugs and back to a life of hope. Each time I deferred, sabotaging the possibility of true freedom.

Why did I recoil from these chances? Because I was a repeat failure. I had given in to cravings so often that going back to drugs felt more familiar than normalcy. Sad but true.

Knowing our flawed efforts are tied to our ability to succeed can be threatening precisely because success lies in our hands. When we don't ask for God's help, which He wants to give us, we have only our limited resources. This increases the risk for self-sabotaging our success to protect ourselves—in case our efforts aren't enough.

Acting out of fear postpones hope. We continue to lack the faith that life can be abundant and better. *It has never come together for me before, so what would be different this time?* That's what I believed when Regina told me about Magdalene, and when I went home to Mama's with my kids.

What I didn't know then, but know now, is that if an open door to hope comes my way and it's God's will, nothing can stop my success. When we embrace hope instead of fear, in whatever difficult or desperate situation we face, our lives will change.

What difference did that make for me? When I finally grabbed the chance to get off the streets, God restored me, forgave me, and blessed me. I now live the dream He gave me so long ago, to be an author and speaker, and to spread the goodness of Jesus.

If you have deferred hope in some way, ask God for a chance to be restored. He's waiting to open that door for you to a hopeful future. "For I know the plans I have for you," declares the LORD, "plans to prosper you and not to harm you, plans to give you hope and a future" (Jeremiah 29:11, NIV).

CHAPTER 7

Substituting Hope

I didn't sleep much during my years of addiction. Crack keeps you up for days on end. But whenever my body finally gave out and I did sleep, I woke with a gnawing belly ache. Sleeping meant no drugs for hours, and stone-cold sobriety offered only physical and mental misery. *I need a wake-up*, was always my first thought when my eyes snapped open.

I continued to look for crack in Nashville, taking occasional trips back to Mama's house. But getting a hit without money got harder and harder. Jobs never lasted beyond the first paycheck because I'd spend everything I made and stop going to work. I wrote bad checks for my tea-length dresses or a hot honey biscuit, but the small relief those provided soon vanished.

One day at Mama's house my brother's friend made me an offer. We used to get high together and help each other get drugs. I knew he had a few rocks of crack in his pocket, and asked if I could have one on credit. "I'll pay you back."

His lip curled up in a sneer. He gave me a look I'd come to know all too well. "No. But I'll give it to you if you sleep with me."

My stomach lurched. The thought of him putting his hands on me made me sick, yet my all-consuming, unquenchable drug craving overcame my disgust. If I had to do this to get high, then I could get through it. *It's just this once. Just a few minutes. Just be quick and I'll get what I need.*

I quickly forgot my humiliation and disgust as soon as the crack took hold. *That wasn't so bad.*

I didn't know I'd opened a door I couldn't close. Without a job, turning tricks became an easy way to make money for drugs. Once I realized how easy I could make a quick buck, I kept on and reassured myself. *It's not so bad.*

I climbed into cars with strangers, rode with them to hotels, trap houses, and family homes. Sometimes I sold myself for a roof over my head, to escape Nashville's relentless summer heat or bone-chilling winter cold. Once the prostitution started, I rarely returned to my mother's house, where my children waited, peering out the window, hoping the next car would bring me home.

Looking back, I can't believe how I disrespected my body. But I was so deep under the ocean of addiction, I couldn't push my head above the water to comprehend my behavior. I made enough money to keep myself high—the only thing that mattered.

Once when I walked out of a crack house, a man stopped me to ask the time. When I lifted my wrist to check my watch, he grabbed me. There in the alley, this stranger held a knife to my neck as he raped me.

After he ran away, I stood frozen on the sidewalk and consoled myself. *At least I didn't die.* That was one of many times I'm thankful I was too high to comprehend what had happened. I wish that had been my only rape, but I lost count. People ask, "Why didn't you report the rape to the police?"

When you're a prostitute, your word doesn't count for much. In the best-case scenario, the police laugh in your face. In the worst, they arrest you for prostitution.

Even though I was terrified of being raped again, my addiction drove my choices. I got in a car with a stranger the very next day because my cravings outweighed my fear.

I became a shell of my former self, barely sleeping or eating, staying up constantly, chasing the next hit. I moved from house to house, staying with a drug buddy or shacking up with a man who would turn out to be toxic.

One year, right before Christmas, Mama gave me a long, flowy dress and coat. I looked almost *too* nice. *Nobody's gonna pick me up in this. I look like I just got out of a church service.* So I cut a big hole in my dress, right in the midsection, to show flesh. Ten steps later, a big car stopped. *It worked!* The man turned out to be the weirdest person I ever got in a car with. And that's saying something.

He drove me to his house north of town. When we arrived, he said, "Get down on the floorboards."

So I did.

He didn't want his wife, who was inside the house, to see me. He went in and came back with money and two bottles of liquor. Then he drove to a drug dealer and bought some drugs, and afterward took me to a hotel in Goodlettsville. Although he and his wife were local business owners, he took the risk of being seen.

I knew the situation wasn't good, but I had determined to do almost anything for my next fix. I'd been in disgusting situations before, but he topped them all. He wanted me to be submissive and made me crawl across the floor to get the crack from him. I stayed all night but couldn't get high because I was so disgusted and upset.

In a strange twist, because he gave me a lot of cash, I gave my kids and mom money that Christmas—for the first time in a long time. Even then I knew the price for looking the streetwalker part had been too high.

The years of addiction, trauma, and abuse took a huge toll on my sense of worth. Over time I lost touch with everything good and decent about me.

I slept and ate little. I rarely bathed. Childhood trauma led to drug use, which progressed to the daily, sometimes hourly, demeaning selling of myself like a commodity. This life stripped away any sense of value I once had. I substituted hope for momentary and constant hits of numbness through drugs and prostitution.

But the drugs weren't the only problem. I lived in a revolving door of going to jail, getting out, returning to jail, getting out, only to return again. I sank into an abhorrent lifestyle and felt my life had lost all meaning, all worth.

I did try to quit with a few twenty- and thirty-day rehab stints. I know now those were half-hearted attempts—I never gave them my full effort. Most of the time I just tried to stay out of jail, although I'd long since lost my fear of getting arrested. I was in and out of the Davidson County Jail for prostitution and drug charges. Everybody on the street knew rehab provided a guaranteed get-out-of-jail card, but since I didn't believe rehab worked, I didn't try.

Then Regina came to jail. While she explained how she'd gotten clean and tried to get me to go to Magdalene , where she worked, I told her there was no use for me to go, because rehab never worked.

She didn't give up but kept talking about the place, which did sound different from other programs that tossed you after thirty days. This women-only, residential program lasted two years. Everybody they accepted got a place to sleep, plenty of food, classes, and therapy to help them heal, and even job training through a place called Thistle Farms. And best of all, it was free.

Despite my outward negative response, something about her description of Magdalene captivated me. Looking at Regina, glowing and happy, I suspected this place and this opportunity might be different.

Maybe they could help me. Maybe I could be normal again.

Before she left, she scribbled her phone number on a slip of paper and pressed it into my hand. "Why don't you give me a call? I can get you in if you decide you want help."

I still had the phone number in my pocket when I was released, but still wasn't ready to call. Not yet. I resisted reaching out in faith again. I'd been substituting crack for hope for too long.

Even so, I had a feeling this number would be important one day. I didn't want to lose the contact like everything else. So the next time I visited my mom and kids, I took a photograph off the wall and scrawled the number on the back. With the photograph safely replaced, I sighed with relief. I could find it if I ever needed it.

What's your substitute? You may fight the same demons I did or battle with another unhealthy pattern of behavior to try to fill a void or numb your pain. Maybe you choose alcohol or shopping or keeping up with the Joneses. But know that whatever you substitute for hope will ultimately rob you of your sense of value.

According to the Word of God, you give up when you put hope aside. The Bible says:

* ⁖ * ⁖ *

HOPE IS ALWAYS REAL

Let us not become weary in doing good, for at the proper time we will reap a harvest if we do not give up.

—Galatians 6:9, NIV

* * * * *

Blessed is the man who remains steadfast under trial, for when he has stood the test he will receive the crown of life, which God has promised to those who love him.

—James 1:12, ESV

* * * * *

Surely there is a future, and your hope will not be cut off.

—Proverbs 23:18, ESV

* * * * *

For whatever was written in former days was written for our instruction, that through endurance and through the encouragement of the Scriptures we might have hope.

—Romans 15:4, ESV

* * * * *

Hold on to these promises. When you seek God to fill your void and give Him your pain, you won't need to find a substitute for hope. You'll have the real deal.

CHAPTER 8

Hope in Bondage

Walking the streets, I had two fears—dying and going to prison. Though I gave no evidence of being a God-fearing woman, I still believed in Him, and cried out to Him almost daily to protect me from those two worst-case scenarios. Sometimes I was too stoned to form my own prayers, and I could only croak out the twenty-third Psalm, which I'd learned as a little girl.

Other times I bargained with God through foxhole prayers—when things were critically bad. "God, if you just get me out of this, I'll go home to White House." God proved faithful and I went home, but I never stayed long. My addiction lured me back to Nashville.

Even at the worst of my drug use, I had not forgotten God was there, and somehow listening to my prayers.

I rarely got angry at God. Maybe I knew not to give Him a piece of my mind for the choices I'd made. Maybe I realized my responsibility for my mess. But one night, I'd had it. I'd slept at a friend's house after staying up for days smoking crack and woke up ravenous. I couldn't remember the last time I'd eaten. My friend said she'd fix me something to eat if I gave her some money, so I handed her my last few dollars and went to sleep.

When I woke up, my stomach ached from hunger as the scent of chicken and potatoes wafted into my room. I marched into the kitchen and reached out to grab a handful, too hungry to bother with a fork. But she grabbed my hand. "That ain't for you." She wouldn't let me have even a crumb.

Furious, I stormed out of the house. Thunder and lightning crackled in the sky as I stared up and hollered as loud as I could. "God, if you're there, why don't you do something!"

I didn't notice the headlights growing brighter as they came closer. The car parked next to the sidewalk and a police officer stepped out. "Miss Walker? You're under arrest."

All my bad checks had finally caught up with me.

The judge sentenced me to nine months at the Tennessee Prison for Women, a much more serious punishment than county jail. My nightmare became my reality. I was literally behind bars, not free to make my own decisions.

To my surprise, the accommodations weren't so bad. I had a bed and regular meals. My aching for crack eventually went away. I was healthy for the first time since I'd hit the streets of Nashville. I now see that in the midst of bondage, God provided a road to freedom.

This *should* have been my turning point. Now that I was clean, I had a second chance. When I walked out of prison with my belongings in a trash bag, I should have headed straight to Mama's house, reconnected with my kids, found a job, and gotten my life back. Instead, I looked in the mirror and sighed. I hated my image with the hundred pounds I'd gained in prison. *If I just do crack for two weeks, I could lose the weight real fast. Then I'll quit.*

But that's not how drugs work. I didn't just pick up where I left off nine months before, but plunged into an addiction that returned with a vengeance. The intensified urge for drugs left me powerless to quit. Crack ruled my life like a dictator, forcing me into a life I hated but couldn't escape.

Crack, like a chain, bound me to what seemed to be a permanent road to destruction. Yet at times, I glimpsed a tiny shred of hope that I could regain the innocence and joy of my early childhood.

Occasionally people said, "You're a good girl deep inside."

But I sure didn't act like one. The powerful beast of addiction kept me constantly hungry for the next hit. Getting high no longer numbed my pain. Now, my escape actually enslaved me. I was terrified I wouldn't have enough money to get high. I decided that if my earnings came from selling my body, I better treat myself like a business.

I kept myself looking good, always in a fresh dress with clean hair. Prostitution was a numbers game, and I intended to play. On a good day, I got in a car with a different man every hour, twelve hours a day. I learned which men were safe and which cars to avoid. Despite my caution, I was raped repeatedly. More than once, I thought my life was over.

Most of the money I made didn't last ten minutes, only long enough to walk to the nearest dealer. I took any leftover cash, wadded it up, and stashed in my bra or wig. I had to be careful because everyone else on the street was desperate too. I didn't know what they might do to get their own hit.

I'll never forget Mama's look of disgust when I showed up at my daughter's high school graduation, so high I could barely walk straight. I considered myself a good mom for showing up, but no one viewed me that way. Sadly, I was too blind to see the world through anybody's eyes but my own. I missed the anguish on my kids' faces, desperate to believe I might still change, but furious that I'd abandoned them. I overlooked the dark circles of fatigue under Mama's eyes from years of sleepless nights, worrying the next phone call would inform her I was dead. She told everybody I was sick, and she was right.

I couldn't see what others clearly saw. I still hadn't hit rock bottom.

We usually can't see our own chains. Bondage is defined as "the state of being a slave; servitude or subjugation to a controlling person or force. "My controlling force was drugs, but controlling forces can come from anywhere—a job, abusive people, money, stress to perform, fear of failure—anything that takes over your life.

The cross sets believers free, wipes the slate of sin clean, and connects us to our God and savior forever. With God, any bondage can be overcome.

Actual bondage (jail, addictions, abuse, unhealthy relationships) or emotional bondage (lack of self-worth, the pain of unhealthy messages from our past) only wields the power over us that we allow. In jail I was physically confined, however, my mind was free. No one could sell me. I didn't have to walk the street or turn tricks. Behind bars, I could rest and be in my own skin.

My addiction constricted every part of my life like physical chains restrict movement. I lost so much, but never stopped praying, never stopped hoping. In a seriously unhealthy relationship, I still prayed and believed. At work, I felt emotional bondage. The enemy crushed my self-worth to defeat me.

Yet our God has and will always defeat the enemy. He breaks our chains. We can always find relief and security in Him. When any bondage sneaks up on me, I cry out to God, "Hide me behind your wings, oh Lord." We are secure beneath His wings.

Our past inflicts another form of bondage. My dad's murder and my abusive husband left deep wounds that bound me in ways I could not break with my own wisdom or strength. Shattering the chains of past hurt is hard but not impossible. The key to freedom from the past is forgiveness—forgiving others and asking for forgiveness for yourself. Only God can truly give us the strength to offer and ask for forgiveness. He quickly responds when we ask; His forgiveness can help us forgive others and ourselves.

Why can't we do this on our own? Because this is a spiritual conflict. "We wrestle not against flesh and blood, but against principalities, against powers, against the rulers of the darkness of this world, against spiritual wickedness in high places" (Ephesians 6:12, KJV). That's why we need supernatural power to succeed and regain freedom. God's Word shows us how to fight this battle:

* ☼ * ☼ *

Finally, be strong in the Lord and in the strength of his might. Put on the whole armor of God, that you may be able to stand against the schemes of the devil. . . . Therefore take up the whole armor of God, that you may be able to withstand in the evil day, and having done all, to stand firm.
—Ephesians 6:10–11, 13

* ☼ * ☼ *

We have to prepare for battle, but we don't fight alone against our chains. When we belong to God through Jesus Christ, the Holy

Spirit works within us, day in and day out, shaping us, molding us, refining in us the image of Jesus, and giving us the power and strength to break whatever binds us.

When the Spirit reveals the devastation ongoing sin causes, we need to admit what sin does to our relationship with God. The separation can only be restored when we confess and forsake the sin that enslaves us. We ask God for forgiveness, then He frees to go and sin no more.

What does freedom feel like? After my release, I could breathe! I could praise! My entire being felt like a fresh spring day after a long rough winter. The breath of the Lord kissed my face. The sun warmed my lips. I sang. I jumped. I shouted. "Hallelujah! No weapons formed against me shall prosper!"

God's freedom reinforces our belief that He keeps His promises and does what He says He will do. If He brought me out of addition and despair, He can bring you out too. His freedom is now and forever more.

*   *   *   *   *

May the God of hope fill you with all joy and peace in believing, so that by the power of the Holy Spirit you may abound in hope.

—Romans 15:13, ESV

*   *   *   *   *

Through him we have also obtained access by faith into this grace in which we stand, and we rejoice in hope of the glory of God.

—Romans 5:2, ESV

CHAPTER 9

Songs of Hope

People on the streets considered me "churchy" because I always sang—usually a gospel song. Music soothed my spirit and gospel singing connected me to good memories of my childhood. That's probably why those melodies flowed from me in such unlikely circumstances.

My dad and mom loved music—well, more accurately, they loved praising the Lord. God gave them the ability to praise Him in the midst of trials and tribulations.

I grew up listening to music in the morning, at noon, and even at midnight. If I had a dime for every hymn or chorus I've sung, I wouldn't be able to count the money.

Dad would come home from the fields—tired, dirty, and worn, but never too tired for his favorite song, "The Lord Will Make a Way Somehow." As soon as he started, I jumped on his lap, held my hands up in the air, and imagined an audience of millions of people, engaging them the way I thought Shirley Temple did. With my hairbrush microphone, I sang and danced for what seemed like hours on end.

HOPE IS ALWAYS REAL

I loved singing with both of my parents, although Mama's consistent off-key voice contrasted to my dad's deep bass. Whenever I heard his mellow vibrato, I got chills.

I made up praise songs and bowed at the end of each one as my imaginary congregation joined me. Yep. Those were the days, singing with all the showmanship and feelings I could muster.

I loved singing with my daddy and wanted to sound just like him. Yet I couldn't figure out how he got his voice to sound all curvy and up and down.

One hot day, while I performed with my hairbrush in front of the mirror, I put my face in front of the fan to cool off. The rushing air made my voice vibrate, almost like a robot, and I thought I'd discovered the secret of Daddy's vibrato style. I didn't know that effect comes from feeling the song.

You might dismiss my recollections. "All that's fine. You sang like any carefree kid."

Remember, I was the child of sharecroppers who only got paid once a year, who worked long hours. I learned how to sing in the hard times when I was young. Music in the midst of hopelessness has always been my way of life.

Music taught me a way to pray from the depths of my soul, saying thank you to God. No doubt those early years of praise and gospel songs stuck with me. I continued to sing them as an addict on the streets   for years. Music and praising God kept me spiritually and emotionally connected to my early life, my father, and my heavenly Father, when I had no other connections besides drug users.

After my arrest for bad checks, I arrived late in the evening at the women's prison. I'd expected to be released from the local jail in Gallatin, Tennessee, to go home. Instead, they transferred me to the Tennessee Prison for Women. Walking into the midst of one of my biggest fears—prison, I found unexpected solace in the security, the steady meals, and a bed.

I also found comfort in music when I joined the TPW praise and worship choir. The chance to sing with that group provided a beautiful break from daily prison routines. While I got clean from drugs, I praised God through song.

I sang all the time. Once I sang from dark to dawn in my cell. When the doorkeeper came to let me out for breakfast, he asked, "How did you get a radio in your cell? I listened to your music all night."

I smiled. "That was me singing to the Lord. No music. No radio. Just me and the Lord." Despite my fears, I never stopped singing God's praises.

That reminded me of the time in Acts 16 when Paul and Silas sang in prison. They had been falsely accused and beaten for breaking Roman law after they cast out demons while spreading the gospel. They were placed in cell with their feet in stocks. Not a likely situation to prompt hours of singing.

Around midnight, as they sang, and the other prisoners listened, suddenly an earthquake rocked the jail, the prison doors flew open, and all the prisoners' chains fell off. Paul and Silas did not run but assured the frightened jailer they were all still there. No doubt, they all wondered what such strange happenings meant.

"Even when no one was in sight, they prayed to the Lord with all their might. Midnight came and all was clear, but then the jailhouse began to rock and reel. The stocks that held to their feet were shaken a loose and they walked out in the street. Didn't I tell you it would be all right" (from "Didn't I Tell You," by Dorothy Norwood, a song I sing in my choir).

Paul and Silas didn't expect an earthquake or to be set free. They sang because they experienced God's internal freedom even while imprisoned. Location didn't matter, because their only real bonds connected them to Jesus Christ. Paul viewed his frequent prison time as an opportunity to praise God and share the gospel no matter where he was.

What imprisons you? We can all have invisible as well as outward chains. Remind yourself that when you sing, others will listen, like the doorkeeper in the Tennessee Prison for Women. Sing and trust God to bring your release at the right time.

Music feeds the soul, uplifting and comforting us. Music brings joy, expresses emotions, and surpasses understanding. When I sing, I experience the presence of God. For me, to sing is to pray, and I am filled with His joy, peace, love, and empowerment.

The Bible commands us to sing praises to the Lord, to come into His presence with singing. Even nature sings praise to the creator. Whether we have solo quality voices or those better suited to the shower or car, scripture commands us to show forth the glory of God in song.

Pray through song and watch God change things.

CHAPTER 10

Prayers of Hope

Every day growing up we had mandatory prayer from morning to night. We prayed when we woke up, blessed every meal—including snacks—and finished up with prayer at bedtime.

Each night I knelt by my bed with my big sister. I imitated the voice of a Southern Baptist preacher with my hand over my forehead and a quiver in my voice. "Thank You, Jesus, for another day. I played and I didn't get hurt. I ate because You gave me food. When I go to sleep, watch over us. See You tomorrow. In Jesus's name. Amen."

At meals, we all said a verse before being allowed to pick up a chicken leg. I usually said, "Jesus swep." Much later I learned the words were, "Jesus wept." Finally, my dad explained the verse and I learned Jesus cried for His friend, which made me sad.

I often played "church" outside. I sang a solo, said a prayer, and of course, shouted the way Mama did *every* Sunday. My hat flew off, my fan fell on the ground, but I kept talking really fast, like she did.

I loved prayer time in Sunday school. When I prayed, I called every student by name. "Bless my brother Lansford, my sister Portia,

James, and Joe Allen, and bless the chicken that mom wrung his head off yesterday, and Lord, please help my dad not to be so tired at night, and help Mama make enough biscuits for everyone in the whole wide world. Amen."

I prayed during the cold months in Tennessee when I sat by the fire. I prayed for new shoes for Easter. All simple childhood prayers.

But during family time, I learned prayer was real, not routine. My parents taught me God listens to His children and answers. Daddy got loud and Mama smiled, but they both believed in the power of prayer—that prayer changes things.

What shocks folks who hear my story is that all the time I spent on the streets—all twenty-six years—I prayed.

The woman you drive by on the streets and think is too far gone—she may be praying too. Me? I learned as a child from Mama and Daddy and I never, ever stopped. Even when I lived through a hell on earth.

I did plenty of foxhole praying. On days and nights when my entire body ached and jerked with that antsy feeling deep inside, my belly empty, I spoke to God like a friend I could bargain with.

"Now, God, You know I'm addicted, You know I'm a mess. They tell me You don't bless no mess, so I'm not asking for a blessing. Just let a car stop and pick me up. I'll take care of the rest. But not an abuser, or a rapist, or someone broke. Just someone to help ease my jonesing. Once I get paid and I get a hit, I'll go home to White House and lay down for a while. I promise."

When somebody came along, I made good on my promise and went home for a bit.

Occasionally I fell short on my side, and landed in jail, or got hung up somehow. That made me paranoid, thinking God would punish me for breaking my word. I even thought I deserved the bad things that happened to me. Doing drugs and selling yourself for money is a dangerous business. *God's letting this happen. That's why that man hit me with the gun handle and ripped me off.* If I broke my promise to God, I thought I deserved the abuse. Those were dark thoughts.

But God doesn't punish His children that way. He's not a God to bargain with. He is Almighty God, but also a loving Father who waits for us to come home to Him, no matter what situation we've created with our sin. Whatever we pray, He wants His children to seek Him, to call out to Him, to talk to Him.

Talking to God brought me relief, no matter what my words were. Even when I made promises I couldn't keep. Prayer reminded me that God saw and heard me in my lowest times.

Sometimes I gave in to despair. I'd cry out in pain.

* ❊ * ❊ *

God, I can't go on anymore. I am nothing! My life will never change. I am trash! No one would ever want me as a wife or even a girlfriend. I've had enough. Let me die, God. I pray You will not send me to hell. I am already living through hell right here on earth.

Please, please, God I don't want to be beat up or treated like a homeless dog anymore. Just come get me. You said I only need the faith of a mustard seed. I'm having faith that You will let me die right now.

* ❊ * ❊ *

I prayed raw, honest words even if they didn't make sense. I wonder now about those addled thoughts, but addicts aren't in their right minds. Even so, I constantly talked to God. Sometimes I told Him how astonished I was to still be alive.

*　*　*　*　*

Heavenly Father, somehow, I'm still alive. Last night two Hispanic guys raped me. I hurt. I'm so shaken, yet I'm relieved. When people have said, "Hallelujah, anyhow," I never knew what they meant. Now I get it! My life is terrible, but You are in charge, saving me in spite of myself. My life was almost snuffed out. They nearly did me in, but Hallelujah anyhow, because I'm still alive.

*　*　*　*　*

Normally stoned out of my mind on crack cocaine, I often couldn't put together coherent words. Scared, bone-tired, I waited in all kinds of weather to be mistreated by the next john to make enough money to get high again. The vicious cycle went from longing for drugs, to shame at what I'd done, to euphoria and energy when the drug hit, and then to deep shame again.

I felt less than human and thought any moment might be my last. Exhausted, I waited to be mistreated, feared for my life, all the while terrified of the dark. I'd grown up in church with a mother who knew the Word, so when I couldn't form prayers, I recited favorite scriptures. On dark nights I said the 23rd Psalm and added my thoughts.

*　*　*　*　*

The Lord is my shepherd; I shall not want.
I am wanting, Lord!

He maketh me to lie down in green pastures.

Where are those pastures, Lord?!

He leadeth me beside the still waters.

This nasty alley is nothing like a pretty stream.

He restoreth my soul. He leadeth me in the paths of right-eousness for his name's sake.

Someday I'll be righteous. Someday.

Yea, though I walk through the valley of the shadow of death,

In crack houses and the dingy, sour-smelling alleys,

I will fear no evil;

I'm fearing now, God. Protect me!

For thou art with me; thy rod and thy staff they comfort me.

Yes, Lord!

Thou preparest a table before me in the presence of mine enemies.

Thou anointest my head with oil; my cup runneth over.

Surely goodness and mercy shall follow me all the days of my life:

and I will dwell in the house of the Lord forever,

God, please. That house of Yours. I want to be there. Please, if You would just please come and see about me, I will always dwell in the house of the Lord forever.

* ⁙ * ⁙ *

I didn't know what "the house of the Lord" meant. Whatever the phrase described, I believed it was the opposite of where I was and what I was doing.

Nobody chooses to become a prostitute and an addict. In fact, knowing few women survive and get out led to my most frequent and audacious prayer: "God take me out of this place. Take me into a new place where I can be happy and normal. Someplace where I'm not relying on criminals and abusers for my next hit or meal or place to sleep. Make me safe and happy."

I didn't have the ability to escape my circumstances, but I hoped that God would do it for me. During this inhuman life, while I walked Meridian Street, Cleveland Street, Dickerson Road, I prayed. Whether in or out of jail, or left in a ditch for dead, I still cried out to the Lord.

What have you been praying? Are you audacious in asking? Would you be nervous or ashamed to share your requests with others? Are your words saturated with despair or hopelessness? Do you have a mustard seed of hope that He is with you?

Maybe, like me, you sometimes don't even have words. The good news is that you can tell Him anything, anywhere. He's always listening and understands your muddled requests. He's holding out a hand to rescue every single one of us. I'm living proof.

When we reach to our heavenly Father out of despair, He hears us. He loves us. The Lord knows every groan from your deepest pain. Our Father wants us to cry out to Him during those desperately lonely times of anguish.

* ⁒ * ⁒ *

When the righteous cry for help,

the LORD *hears and delivers them out of all their troubles.*

The LORD *is near to the brokenhearted*

and saves the crushed in spirit.

Many are the afflictions of the righteous,

but the LORD *delivers him out of them all.*

He keeps all his bones;

not one of them is broken.

—Psalm 34:17–20, ESV

* ❄ * ❄ *

Yet darkness brings hopelessness, and we wonder why we should pray. "If you're going to worry, then why pray? If you are going to pray, then why worry?" This saying reminds us that prayer changes things. You can pray your way out of hopelessness. That's why the Bible reminds us to pray continually.

* ❄ * ❄ *

Rejoice in hope, be patient in tribulation, be constant in prayer.

—Romans 12:12, ESV

* ❄ * ❄ *

Rejoice always, pray without ceasing, give thanks in all cir-cumstances; for this is the will of God in Christ Jesus for you.

—1 Thessalonians 5:16–18. ESV

* ❄ * ❄ *

Do not be anxious about anything, but in everything by prayer and supplication with thanksgiving let your requests be made known to God.

—Philippians 4:6, ESV

* ❄ * ❄ *

And whatever you ask in prayer, you will receive, if you have faith.

—Matthew 21:22, ESV

* ❄ * ❄ *

Because God has promised to answer our prayers, when we go to Him to pray, we need to remember that we aren't trying to change His mind or bend His will to ours. He knows what is best for us, and His timing is always perfect, no matter when or how He answers. He is always faithful to keep His promises.

* ❄ * ❄ *

Then you will call on me and come and pray to me, and I will listen to you.

—Jeremiah 29:12

* ❄ * ❄ *

Therefore I tell you, whatever you ask in prayer, believe that you have received it, and it will be yours.

—Mark 11:24

* ❄ * ❄ *

Authentic prayer comes from the deepest part of the soul, relies on the promises of God, and knows He is faithful. God has whatever you need. Search the Word, believe the promises, and receive His answer.

Why did I pray while addicted? I felt heard. I knew God knew me, because I had been talking to Him all my life. If I asked God for protection, I knew He'd spare me—even by landing me in jail.

So every day I offered the same request. "Protect me. Help me. Hide me behind Your wings."

My daddy often said, "The Lord will make a way somehow." Every day I heard his voice in my head. I loved and trusted my dad who introduced me to God, and his faith sustained me for a while.

When I met God for myself—that was a game changer. I went from knowing God through the eyes of my parents to believing because of what He did for me.

As you pray for hope, meditate on these Bible verses to help you recall the faithfulness of God.

* ⁘ * ⁘ *

Let us hold unswervingly to the hope we profess, for he who promised is faithful.
—Hebrews 10:23, NIV

* ⁘ * ⁘ *

But those who hope in the LORD will renew their strength.

They will soar on wings like eagles;

they will run and not grow weary,

they will walk and not faint.

—Isaiah 40:31, NIV

* ❋ * ❋ *

But the eyes of the LORD *are on those who fear him,*

on those whose hope is in his unfailing love.

—Psalm 33:18, NIV

* ❋ * ❋ *

May the God of hope fill you with all joy and peace as you
trust in him, so that you may overflow with hope by the power
of the Holy Spirit.

—Romans 15:13, NIV

* ❋ * ❋ *

And hope does not disappoint, because the love of God has been
poured out within our hearts through the Holy Spirit who was
given to us.

—Romans 5:5, NET

* ❋ * ❋ *

A Prayer for Hope

Lord, I maintain my hope in You and I hold on to
the assurance that what I am praying for is already accom-
plished in the name of Jesus. Your Word
promises "no good thing does He withhold from those who

walk uprightly" (Psalm 84:11, ESV). I wait upon You for Your definition of the "good thing" You will not withhold from me. As David prayed, "I love you, Lord, my strength. The Lord is my rock, my fortress and my deliverer; my God is my rock, in whom I take refuge, my shield and the horn of my salvation, my stronghold" (Psalm 18:1, NIV).

* ⁜ * ⁜ *

I knew if I prayed and God had mercy on my soul and spared my life, I would be made whole. God answered my most audacious prayer. He gave me a whole new world and a good, good life. My own story still blows my mind, and I'm forever grateful and so blessed to share it with you.

CHAPTER 11

Hope Resurrected

A year and a half went by and Regina's phone number remained untouched on the back of my daughter's picture at Mama's house. I hadn't set foot there since that day. But something kept tugging at me, telling me to call my mom, to let her know I was still alive.

Street life exhausted me more than a hit could fix. My bones felt weary, my mind overwhelmed, and my body too sluggish to get up and hustle. I'd become the woman I hated, sitting in a crack house, begging for a crumb.

So when Mama asked me to come home and sing at her church choir's twenty-fifth anniversary, I said yes. Lying in my childhood bedroom, I rested for the first time in months, but all I could think about was that phone number in the next room.

Without a telling a soul, I called Regina. My hands shook. "I can't do this no more. I want to come to your program."

Her response hit me like a gut punch.

"Dorris, that's great, but you'll have to be patient. Magdalene has a waiting list of 150 people. But don't give up." Admission could be weeks, even months, she told me. While I worried that I couldn't hold out that long, she made me a deal. "If you call me every day, and stay off the streets, I promise I'll figure out a way to get you in."

She offered me a glimmer of hope.

So I stayed at my mom's. I rehearsed with the choir, and the morning of the anniversary, led the whole church in the gospel song "You're Looking at a Miracle." By then I was rested. I was fed. The streets didn't sound so bad anymore.

I could hear my mom rattling the house with fervent prayers for me, begging the Lord to keep me home. Even her prayers couldn't stop me from packing my few belongings to head out. When the phone rang, I figured I had a ride back to Nashville. Instead, my heart leaped at Regina's voice. "We have room for you."

A miracle happened, just like the song.

On November 9, 2009, my brother dropped me off at the most beautiful house I'd ever seen—unlike any rehab center or halfway house in my experience. *These people really gonna let somebody like me stay here?*

When I walked inside, I saw a woman curled up on a sofa and my body got tense. Until now, women had been my competition, not my friends. They stood between me and my next payday.

She smiled and welcomed me. "Hi, I'm Sonya. Some days here are better than others." Her big brown eyes stared into mine. "No matter what, just stick and stay."

Her words touched me deep in my spirit, and played over and over in my mind. *Stick and stay,* as I relearned how to go to bed at night, get up in the morning, and take a shower.

Stick and stay. I mentally echoed the words while shuttled to Narcotics Anonymous classes and therapy appointments.

Stick and stay came easier than I expected. Instead of pointing fingers and demanding to know what I did, the ladies at Magdalene looked at me with compassion.

I had stepped into a new life. My old world of chaos—days without eating or sleeping, caring only about my next hit, wishing I could change, but not knowing how—was gone.

Now I lived within a routine. I enjoyed three meals a day and slept in a soft bed with clean sheets every night. The simplest pleasures took me by surprise. I'll never forget the first morning I woke up in my own bed to see sunlight streaming through my window. When I joined other ladies on the back porch, I was overwhelmed by the music of birds chirping in the trees. After years of staying up night after night on the street, I never noticed the birds. Now they were here, serenading me over breakfast.

I dove head-first into my recovery. I had classes each day that taught me how drugs impacted not just my own body and life but also the lives of my family and friends. I attended Narcotics Anonymous meetings and talked with a counselor. I figured she would scold me about my past, for making destructive decisions and wasting my life. Instead, she looked me straight in the eyes and asked, "What happened to you?"

Slowly I realized what she was asking me. She didn't want to know what happened on the streets; she wanted to know about *me*. For the first time in decades, I understood that the trauma of Daddy's brutal death was behind my addiction. I finally knew it wasn't all my fault, that no one wakes up one day and says, "I want to be a prostitute." At that moment I believed there was hope for my future.

She told me if I took one step, she'd do the rest. She even handed me a key to the house. Nobody'd trusted me like that in twenty-six years.

One day my counselor asked me to write down three goals. I thought hard, then listed the most far-fetched goals I could imagine: "Get an apartment. Buy a car. Be normal."

Even off the streets, feeling normal took a while. When I was with the other women, I had nothing to talk about but drug stories and turning tricks. I didn't know myself off crack. Not only did I learn to live clean; I discovered how to think differently and redis-covered my own personality. I did the work. I peeled back the layers. I found myself without the drugs, the chaos, the streets. Magdalene offered me a brand-new life I was head-over-heels crazy about.

On weekends, I got to visit my mom and children. I couldn't wait to walk into Mama's house with my arms full of sweet-smelling soaps, lotions, and perfumes I received from Thistle Farms. I handed the bag to my mom. "You can give these out as Christmas presents." Af-ter all the years of Mama giving me so much, I could finally give her something.

After a while, Thistle Farms gave me a job. In addition to oper-ating Magdalene, Thistle Farms also runs a global enterprise of home and spa products and accessories, to offer the women they help work experience as part of their recovery. I now had a real job.

I focused hard to keep my knees from knocking together when I first stepped onto the workroom floor, a place thick with the scent of lavender. My first job in years was pouring lip balm into tiny pots, when I didn't have a craftsman's bone in my body. They trusted me with this job so I wouldn't let them down. Working fifteen hours a week was part of my treatment program, a way to gain experience so I could eventually get a full-time job.

I made $140 every two weeks—enough for my cell phone bill and a little for savings. I was so proud. For the first time in twenty-six years, I didn't run out and spend every last cent on a hit. That felt good. So I kept going. I rolled up my sleeves and became the best lip-balm maker I could.

Before long they promoted me to running the packing department and making sure the products were sorted in bins so Magdalene graduates could take them when they went out telling their stories.

I had to hit rock bottom in that crack house, with no money or food. I made one last deal with God before I was ready to walk through the door of a chance for a restored life and resurrected hope.

Real hope is found in our creator. If we want Him to redeem our lives when we are lost in fear and darkness and sin, we need to repent and be willing for God to mold us into what He wants us to be and do. That's where I finally found myself; I knew I couldn't live one second longer or take one more step without His help. When we return to God, we find hope and joy.

When we are ready to seek the Father's help, we can often find His love in those who are doing God's work, those who are committed to being the hands and feet of God. I found my way back because of my friend Regina, who introduced me to Magdalene and Thistle Farms.

I was broken, lonely, sad, and didn't know how to live. Thistle Farms gave me a place to live for two years—free. They provided therapy, replaced my teeth, and gave me a job.

Becca Stevens is the founder and president of this amazing community. She taught me so much and gave me opportunities I never thought possible.

I have traveled with Becca. I learned to make and sell our amazing products. Most of all, I learned to tell my story to others who need real hope from God. Through speaking to others, I discovered the power of reliving what God saw me through. I learned to listen to Him and ask Him to speak through me, to allow me to be present and feel His glory and power.

When we meet those in need, as the women in Magdalene met me that day in November 2009, we only need offer the simplest of human kindnesses. We open our doors. We love them until they can love themselves. We freely give, as Jesus said, to do unto others as you would have them do unto you.

When I finally sought God's hope and no longer held on to false hope, I found the promises in the Word to be true. Let these verses from the Father's message of love to us bring you real hope—for yourselves and for others.

* ❋ * ❋ *

Let no one deceive you with empty words, for because of these things the wrath of God comes upon the sons of disobedience.
—Ephesians 5:6, ESV

* ❋ * ❋ *

Rejoice in hope, be patient in tribulation, be constant in prayer.
—Romans 12:12, ESV

* ❋ * ❋ *

Hope deferred makes the heart sick, but a desire fulfilled is a tree of life.
—Proverbs 13:12, ESV

＊ ＊ ＊ ＊ ＊

But in your hearts honor Christ the Lord as holy, always being prepared to make a defense to anyone who asks you for a reason for the hope that is in you; yet do it with gentleness and respect.

—1 Peter 3:15, ESV

＊ ＊ ＊ ＊ ＊

Now faith is the assurance of things hoped for, the conviction of things not seen.

—Hebrews 11:1, ESV

＊ ＊ ＊ ＊ ＊

But test everything; hold fast what is good.

—1 Thessalonians 5:21, ESV

＊ ＊ ＊ ＊ ＊

Real hope will always line up with the Word of God. It will feed and nourish our souls and we will be able to hear God's voice.

CHAPTER 12

Healing Hope

I looked forward to celebrating my next birthday in a new place, but the day before, bad news rocked my world. My hands shook when my sister's words cracked my life apart. "Mama had a stroke." She choked on the words and sobbed. I closed my eyes and the room spun.

My mom spent the last three decades loving me and praying for me when others had given up. She took care of my kids when I failed them. She helped keep me alive, and was the reason I was at Magdalene. Now, well into her nineties, she was gone, dying peacefully in her sleep.

The world that had finally started to look bright and cheerful suddenly went dark again. Deep depression settled over me. I could barely get out of bed, much less drag myself to therapy or classes. My recovery slammed to a halt.

Calling a dealer and getting high to numb the pain would have been easy—but I couldn't go back. Mama wouldn't want me to blow my only chance to get better. No matter how hard it was to continue to make the right choice, I had to keep going for her.

One night, a local church had some of us from Magdalene over as guests of honor for a spaghetti dinner. The end made the night especially memorable. As we walked out the door, each of us received a copy of *Jesus Calling* by Sarah Young, signed by every young person at the church. I began reading a meditation from the book every single morning. I hadn't been a reader before, but every day, it seemed the author crawled inside my head, learned about my problems and struggles, and wrote just to me.

With each page, the God I knew as a child seemed to draw me near to Him. He was the true Father I'd longed for, the only one who could fill the hole my dad left, the only one who could heal my guilt for how I'd hurt my kids. Even in the pain after my mom's death, the Lord called me to Him, claiming me as His daughter.

Faith had always been part of my life, but I realized I'd treated God like a vending machine in the sky. Aside from desperate prayers for protection, I never depended on Him or asked Him to be my savior, my Lord, my deliverer. For decades, I sought to fill the hole in my soul from Daddy's death with substance abuse, when only my heavenly Father could restore me. In the quiet of my bedroom that night, I lifted my voice and surrendered to the Lord. I know Jesus is the reason I'm more than a decade clean today.

Slowly I pushed forward. I returned to classes and therapy. Getting through my deep grief in the days after Mama passed was another part of healing. I discovered God's help in a new way. He'd kept me alive all the years on the streets. He'd brought me to this transformative place of redemption, where I was reclaiming hope. He'd shown me I could live clean and enjoy a productive life, learning to trust others. Now He carried me in His arms while I mourned Mama and grieved without drugs.

Recovery is messy and complicated—not a straight line. While I healed from my physical addiction, I had twenty-six years of behaviors, patterns, and ingrained thoughts to unlearn. Once when I had a bill due and no money, my first inclination was to call a man I knew liked me and let him pay me for sex. Gratefully I didn't succumb to that temptation. I had always ended up in relationships with men I didn't care for simply because they gave me money; that was my life for decades. I couldn't think differently overnight. Old patterns took time to unlearn. They took prayer. They took God's deliverance.

Then in 2011, after two years of work, I walked across the stage, and the director hugged me as she handed me my graduation certificate. My daughter and grandchildren cheered in the crowd. It felt like a dream. I clutched the paper and grinned so hard my face hurt! I looked at my daughter and knew I'd never go back to the streets.

All my fears and doubts that I could stay clean and live a different life were erased when I saw my name on that certificate. Two years clean. I had a job—Thistle Farms promoted me to director of events. I no longer feared running out to find the nearest drug dealer. I knew the Lord had delivered me from my addiction and prepared me for life on my own. I was ready to be normal.

This moment was pivotal, but my lessons weren't over. I discovered that no triumph comes without struggles.

I knew I was different, but others weren't so sure. I had to show an apartment manager my certificate from Magdalene before she'd let somebody with my criminal background and measly work history sign a lease. Even though my son furnished my apartment with beautiful, high-quality wood furniture, he wouldn't come over, not even for Thanksgiving dinner. His pain from my abandonment still lingered.

Then another difficult revelation required more healing.

Becca Stevens, our Thistle Farms community founder, often said, "The common thread we all share is that we all have experienced rape between the age of seven and eleven."

That's not part of my story, so why am I here if I haven't experienced the same thing as my other sisters?

I thought I was different for the first three years of my recovery, until I visited a church in June 2012, where a childhood friend and classmate was the pastor. I hadn't seen him for years.

He gave me a big smile and told me how proud he was that I'd gone through the program successfully, gotten clean, and had a job. I felt good to be congratulated and not condemned.

He gave me an innocent hug. I was so happy until a horrible memory hit me in the pit of my stomach and made my limbs tremble.

Not him—not *this* old friend—but *his brother* had molested me when I was a very young—not between seven and eleven, but around four or five. The rush of that memory froze me. For long moments I stood and recalled the experience—the sweaty smell of his brother's body, the beautiful smile he gave my parents. They thought he was a good guy. My mom fed him at our table, and my dad paid him to work in the tobacco fields.

Because he was "such a good guy," he told my mom, "I'll take Dorris and help her wash her hands too."

We went to our wash basin where there was a pitcher of water and soap and washed our hands.

Then he whispered, "Raise your top up."

And I did.

"Give me a kiss."

And I did.

"Give me a hug."

And I did.

As I remember what happened next, I cringed. I *had* been molested as a child by a family friend. That made me feel dirty and angry. I belonged in every way to this sisterhood of battered women.

Even though that painful revelation required more time in counseling, I knew I wouldn't return to drugs or the streets again. I leaned into my beautiful relationship with God to get through.

No matter where we are in our healing journeys, the road we travel curves and we can't always see around the bend. Life still throws us for a loop as the enemy lies in wait to trip us, placing potholes of disappointment and temptation to make us stumble. In those moments we discover how serious our walk with God is. He challenges our faith and at the same time strengthens us.

On this side of the eternal Jordan river, we'll have trials and tribulations. But don't worry or fret for God will never leave us or forsake us.

When trouble comes, the enemy storms in to try and steal our joy, just as he tempted Eve in the garden and later Jesus in the wilderness by twisting God's words.

First, he uses a physical desire. He pointed to fruit for Eve and suggested Jesus turn stones to bread. He may tempt us with drugs or alcohol, food or sex.

Next, he uses material possessions. Eve thought the fruit was pleasing to see. Satan tried to tempt Jesus with the kingdoms of this world. For me, besides money for crack, I focused on my dresses and wigs, so I could feel more like a lady.

Finally, he appeals to our pride, to think we can do anything on our own. Eve faced her failure when God came looking for her, but

Jesus relied on His Father. And for twenty-six years I tried to fix myself.

As a daughter of the heavenly Father, you don't belong to the enemy and his tricks. And you have the power of the Holy Spirit to bring full healing—mind, body, and soul.

When trials and storms come, and you need another level of healing like I did, remain steadfast in the Word of God. Pray continually and move forward toward the future God has promised you.

* * * * *

Not that I have already obtained this or am already perfect, but I press on to make it my own, because Christ Jesus has made me his own. Brothers, I do not consider that I have made it my own. But one thing I do: forgetting what lies behind and straining forward to what lies ahead, I press on toward the goal for the prize of the upward call of God in Christ Jesus. Let those of us who are mature think this way, and if in anything you think otherwise, God will reveal that also to you.

—Philippians 3:12–15, ESV

* * * * *

Do not be conformed to this world, but be transformed by the renewal of your mind, that by testing you may discern what is the will of God, what is good and acceptable and perfect.

—Romans 12:2, ESV

* * * * *

*Continue steadfastly in prayer, being watchful in it with
thanksgiving. At the same time, pray also for us, that God may
open to us a door for the word, to
declare the mystery of Christ, on account of which I am in
prison—that I may make it clear, which is how I ought to
speak. Walk in wisdom toward outsiders, making the best use
of the time. Let your speech always be gracious, seasoned with
salt, so that you may know how you ought to answer each person.*

—Colossians 4:2–6, ESV

* ☼ * ☼ *

If we live by the Spirit, let us also walk by the Spirit.

—Galatians 5:25, ESV

* ☼ * ☼ *

*Therefore, since we are surrounded by so great a cloud of wit-
nesses, let us also lay aside every weight, and sin which clings
so closely, and let us run with endurance the race that is set before us.*

—Hebrews 12:1, ESV

* ☼ * ☼ *

*For it is God who works in you, both to will and to work for
his good pleasure.*

—Philippians 2:13, ESV

* ☼ * ☼ *

For the word of the cross is folly to those who are
perishing, but to us who are being saved it is the power of God.

—1 Corinthians 1:18, ESV

God hears our cries for healing, and He's always right on time.
Just remember, His help is on the way, like the old gospel song says:

* ☼ * ☼ *

I don't know when, but God's gonna do it.

I don't know how, but He's gonna make it.

I don't know where, but God's gonna work it.

I believe it 'cause it's already done!

CHAPTER 13

New Horizons of Hope

Compared to my past, I lived a beautiful life. As director of events for Thistle Farms, I traveled around the country sharing my story, still wearing my signature tea-length dresses. I lived in my own apartment, checking off the first of my three goals. But my son still stayed away.

Slowly my addictive inclinations faded. I no longer had to remind myself not to act or think a certain way. And people noticed—including my son. Six years into my recovery, he showed up on my doorstep, ready to have dinner with me, just the two of us. After that, we were inseparable.

Sometimes I had to stop and pinch myself to make sure I was really awake, that this really was my life. Each morning when my alarm buzzed, I sprang out of bed, bursting to start my day.

God replaced my broken dreams with new ones. I never thought I'd be speaking in front of groups of people. That little girl with the hairbrush microphone might have believed what was happening, but I had a hard time believing what God had done. He gave me another chance, established a relationship with my kids and grandbabies, and allowed me to travel the country telling anybody and everybody about the important work Thistle Farms was doing.

The organization's founder, Becca Stevens, became my close friend and took me under her wing, bringing me with her on television shows and to national landmarks. I'll never forget the moment I stood next to her on the shore of the ocean, the salty breeze spraying in my face. To think all that beauty had been there the whole time and I'd never seen it—that blew my mind.

The day we walked the front steps of the national White House together, I looked at Becca and laughed. Who would have thought I would go from White House, Tennessee, to a crack house, to *the* White House?

One of my goals when I first entered Magdalene was "to be normal." But who can define normal? I was living far beyond what I'd dreamed of on the streets—a life much more thrilling that I ever imagined.

With all God had given me, I felt selfish asking Him for one more thing. But at night, when I lay my head on my pillow and closed my eyes, I ached to have somebody lying next to me, protecting me, keeping me warm and safe.

I prayed with every fiber of my being. *God, please send me a husband.* I knew this was a tall order. I couldn't marry just any man. I needed somebody gentle, somebody who wouldn't scare me the way many men had. I needed somebody who would look beyond my past and see me for the daughter of God I was now.

My relationship picker was broken, so I asked God to pick a man for me who loves God more than he'll ever love me. One who speaks softly and gently and is kind yet strong. One who loves God. One who obeys God, and therefore would treat me as a queen.

God. Did. Just. That!

One day I saw James Taylor at church. He wasn't a stranger—I grew up with him. We called him Jaybird back then. I knew he'd married and had children, that his wife had been an addict, and that she'd passed away.

My heart pounded as he greeted me, shaking my hand with a glimmer in his eye. "You look good, Dorris," he said kindly. *Could it be, God?* My mind raced. Before I knew it, he called and asked me to go the movie *Black Panther*.

While our first date wasn't the stuff dreams are made of—I fell asleep—it started something only God could have designed. James helped me heal in ways I didn't know I needed, and helped me stop seeing relationships with men as transactions, and to trust somebody fully again.

The day he proposed, I thanked God over and over as I held him close. I didn't deserve this wonderful answer, but in God's eyes, I was worth it.

On the worst day of my life, I watched my father die and my mother cry in excruciating pain. The neighbor up the road—Mr. Robert Taylor—came down to our house, touched my brother on the shoulder, and said, "Now you're the man of the house, and you must take care of your sisters and your mom."

Mr. Taylor's daughter was Linda.

Linda was one of my childhood friends.

Linda's brother was a little guy everyone called Jaybird. He was my brother's best friend.

I am amazed how God looked at my past and knew who would and would not accept me. And He brought me little Jaybird, who isn't little anymore, who stands tall and serves God. His name is James Taylor and he is my husband.

I sold myself and got high for twenty-six years in a ten-block radius in Nashville—when I wasn't in jail. I prayed God would give me another world and He did. I think about the children of Israel who were enslaved and then brought out. They wandered the wilderness for years, sometimes ready to give up. God was present for them too, even when they were faithless. My life has been like that. I made it through. Now I'm in the Promised Land.

Today I work in Nashville—the same city where I was trapped for so many years. Now my work has meaning and purpose. I have a home and family in the same little town of White House where I grew up, but it's a different world. A beautiful one. The Promised Land. I live a redeemed life. I love it.

EPILOGUE

Music still remains an integral part of my life—as I speak about Thistle Farms, as I worship God both privately and with others in church. Prior to the pandemic I sang with the senior choir, the Divine Inspiration choir, and the youth choir at my church. I love, love, love leading songs and telling others about the Holy Spirit while praising Good.

I have written countless songs and somehow managed to put them to music without knowing the first thing about a music note. When I'm on the road to speak about Thistle Farms, I have a song I wrote called "I'm a Thistle Farmer," which names every product we make!

But mostly my heart lies in gospel music and sometimes when I tell my story, I sing.

"Amazing Grace," a song I learned and loved as a child, is one I still love to share with others. Music was part of my faith and hope foundation all of my life. God used songs to support me, keep me focused on Him, and despite my street life, be a witness through the years as I sang wherever I was.

For over ten years I've been clean and sober. I travel the country, speaking to crowds and surprising them with my story. Soon they grasp that prostitution *is* common. Drug addiction *is* common. What's not common is making it out alive. And perhaps they wonder, *How does a person fall that low? Could that happen to me?*

I'm here to tell you addiction happens to those you least expect. It happened to me as a perfectly happy twelve-year old girl who loved Jesus and loved singing in church. But the good news is, no one is beyond redemption. Hope is always real with God.